Published by Clink Street Publishing 2018

Copyright © 2018

First edition.

ISBN:
978-1-912850-27-3 - paperback
979-1-912850-28-0 - ebook

About The author

S.J. BAILLIE was born in 1972 in Edinburgh. An avid gardener with an interest in history, architecture and antiques.

The Private World of Cammo was his first book, after which a career in the property industry followed after living abroad.

A period as an art dealer allowed him to expand his interest in antique paintings and researching their provenance.

This revised edition has allowed further information along with a greater range of photographs depicting the history of Cammo House.

August 2017

To my father Eddie…
who gave me the "kick" of encouragement…

To my mother for her support…

Acknowledgements

The National Trust for Scotland, in particular Ian Riches and Marcin Klimek

Historic Environment Scotland

National registers of Scotland

Edinburgh Archaeological Field Society

Capital Collections

Paul Hogarth and Company

Harry Ward – *The Forgotten Greens of Scotland*

Bruce Mickel – Mactaggart & Mickel

Robert Murray Stamps

Tony Acosta – Olivewood Memorial Park, Riverside, CA, US

Authoright

Johnston Press

Frank McLuskie

Friends of Cammo

Contents

Foreword

1989 was a memorable year:

The World Wide Web was invented.

The Berlin Wall came down.

These are only two of the major events in this year... but for me it was discovering Cammo.

It was during a walk with a neighbour and his dog that my lifelong fascination began.

Seeing the remains on a bitterly cold January day, the sunlight casting shadows from tree branches on the stonework, I could never imagine the depth of knowledge and information I would gain.

This journey would take in organised archives, vast libraries and damp storage rooms of files, sifting through plans, old photos and visiting the other side of the world!

In 1995 The Private World of Cammo was published, and now 23 years later a revised edition has been completed.

In all that time my interest and fascination has never diminished.

Cammo House in its heyday, c.1896. NTS

Introduction

I paid my first visit to Cammo in 1989, on a bitterly cold day in January. The reason for my visit was that I was with my neighbour and his dog. My neighbour had told me of a place where he often took the dog for a walk near Cramond Brig and, knowing of my interest in the countryside, he said I would find this place fascinating. How right he was. Although he had said it was near Cramond Brig, I was not very familiar with the area. We arrived and parked the car. I was initially amazed at the extent of the land. We walked past the shell of the Gate Lodge and up the drive towards the house. I can remember standing there and looking at what was left and thought that Cammo had been nothing more than a large country cottage with a rather grand name. While walking around the ground, I asked many questions about Cammo. Who lived there? What happened to the house? Who owned it now? To satisfy my curiosity I decided to pay a visit to the Edinburgh Central Library at George IV Bridge. I found copies of press cuttings from 1977 regarding the fires and a cutting from 1949 regarding Mrs Maitland-Tennent's battle with the Treasury over funds she deposited in America before the war. While there I also came across an early photograph of Cammo, which was featured in a book containing other photographs of houses in the Lothians.

I was astounded by the size of the house pictured and could not believe that it was the same building. After finding these items my interest diminished and my copies were put away in a file and looked at periodically. However, I subsequently became increasingly interested in Cammo and decided to find out as much as I could about its history.

One day I phoned the National Trust for Scotland and asked if they could provide any information about Cammo. I became very excited when I was told that they had many photographs showing the interior and exterior of the house as it was when National Trust staff first went to see it. Two days later photographic slides arrived. It was a Saturday morning and I was so excited at seeing them that I could not eat any breakfast. It may sound rather strange for a grown man to get excited about such things, but Cammo has a very special place in my heart, so I sat down, turned on the projector and viewed the slides one at a time. One of the slides showed a picture of the interior of the drawing room. I suddenly felt very emotional as I gazed at the appalling condition of the fine furnishings and décor. The sheer waste of the house suddenly started to affect me quite deeply and as I viewed other slides of further rooms I was simply stunned. More slides showing the grounds featured rusting cars and outbuildings which have since disappeared.

After this my interest grew and grew. I paid numerous visits to the Royal Commission on the Ancient and Historical Monuments of Scotland, West Register House, Register House and Historic Scotland. I found myself gathering more and more information, maps and photographs than I ever imagined. I visited the National Trust's archives and found myself looking through many files and documents, containing everything from legal matters and proposed development ideas to surveyors' reports. Everything I needed was there, apart from personal information about the Maitland-Tennent family. This was where my new friends were to come in, the Littles.

John's father, Neil, was the tenant farmer at the time of Mrs Maitland-Tennent's death in 1955, and had been for a number of years. He had known the family very well. They told me the tales that lay behind the articles in the newspapers: what Percy was like and the problems he had with thieves, the background about Robert and information about the family's disagreements. It was at this point that I realised that I should share all the knowledge I had gathered and that it would be beneficial to put it in print and to dispel the myths and rumours surrounding Cammo.

Cammo House – A Brief History

The first recorded note about Cammo appears in the mid-fourteenth century, when the land belonged to the Abbot of Inchcolm. By the beginning of the next century, Cammo had passed to the Bishop of Dunkeld, who gave it to John De Nudre in exchange for the tower 'within Cramond' along with land 'within the Barony of Kirk Cramond'.

Later, in the fifteenth centry, a lady of the Niddrie family, Elizabeth, married William Mowbray of the family associated with Barnbogle Castle near South Queensferry.

John Mowbray sold Cammo in 1637 to William Wilkie, an Edinburgh merchant. His granddaughter Rachel married John Menzies of Coulterallers, Lanarkshire, in 1679, and it was he who employed builder Robert Mylne to build a house at Cammo in 1693.

In 1710 Sir John Clerk bought Cammo and resided there until 1723. While at Cammo, Sir John constructed dykes and enclosures and carried out extensive tree planting. Sir John was the leading Scottish landscape designer of his day. One of the most impressive features which can still be seen at Cammo is the man-made knoll situated next to the water tower.

The next resident was John Hog of Berwickshire, who commissioned drawings from William Adam for a major rebuilding project which was never started.

In 1741 John Hog's son sold Cammo for £4252 10s to James Watson of Saughton, Edinburgh. James Watson was married to Helen Hope, whose father was the first Earl of Hopetoun. James had a sale of artefacts from the house in 1742. These consisted of furniture and other household items:

SALE OF FURNITURE: consisting of

Standing beds, feather beds, tapestry chairs, tables, mirrors of different kinds, good collection of prints, five marble tables, marble vases, four figurines of marble representing the 'Judgement of Daisies' by Senior Fugirini and a few marble bustes.

Then, in 1778, while visiting his mistress, Rachel Porteous, James collapsed and died in her kitchen at her home in nearby Corstorphine.

James Watson's son Charles (born in 1740 at Kings Cramond), who married Lady Margaret Carnegie in 1780, inherited Cammo on the death of his father.

In 1842, Helen, the Watson heir, loyally flew a flag from the roof of Cammo House (which had by now been renamed New Saughton) when Queen Victoria visited the Rosebery family at Dalmeny House near South Queensferry.

Then, in 1844, Helen Watson married Sholto Watson-Douglas, 20th Earl of Morton, whose seat was Dalmahoy House, near Edinburgh. Their son, Lord Aberdour, gave up New Saughton in 1873 because he was given Hatton House (destroyed by fire in 1952), which adjoined Dalmahoy.

The next resident was Alexander Campbell, a brewer from 6 Charlotte Square, Edinburgh, who, once he had bought New Saughton and the surrounding estate, changed its name back to the original one of Cammo. It is rumoured that Robert Louis Stevenson visited Cammo and was inspired to use Cammo as the basis for the 'House of Shaws' in *Kidnapped*. Distances mentioned in the book correspond to the distance between South Queensferry and Cammo. It has, however, been difficult to find any concrete evidence to support this claim.

After Alexander Campbell's death his trustees sold Cammo to Mrs Margaret Louisa Clark-Tennent, who had rented the house for a year before buying it in 1896 for the sum of £12,000.

In 1910 Mrs Clark-Tennent was divorced (which was not socially acceptable at the time) and afterwards she and her youngest son Percival became 'recluses'. Her eldest son, Robert, stayed in America. After her divorce Mrs Clark-Tennent changed her name to Maitland-Tennent. The reason for taking the name Maitland is unclear. She died in 1955, aged 95, having lived most of her life at Cammo. She bequeathed the estate to her son Percival.

However, by this time the house was very run down and neglected, and after Percival's death in 1975 the empty house fell victim to vandals and thieves. Twice in 1977 the house was ravaged by fire and subsequently it was semi-demolished in 1979 and again in 1980.

The National Trust for Scotland (which had been bequeathed the house by Percival Maitland-Tennent) gifted the estate by feu charter to Edinburgh District Council, which founded a wildlife park and open space for the people of Edinburgh.

Postcard view of Cammo, with carriage at the entrance, c.1900. NTS

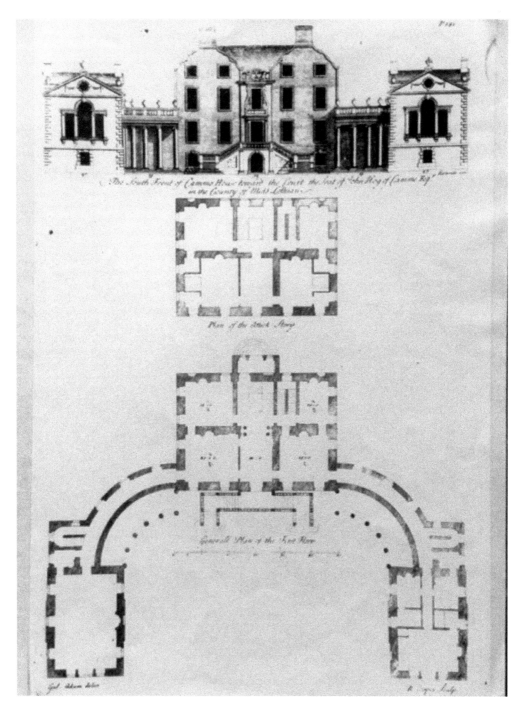

John Hog's proposed alterations as shown in William Adam's Vitruvius Scoticus c.1724. the scheme was never carried out. HES

The Building of Cammo

In 1693 when John Menzies built the original house it was believed to resemble Prestonfield House.

The front of the house faced south-east with the south-west wall overlooking parkland. The house was arranged on three floors including a large basement. The main front had a symmetrically placed, central broken stone pediment doorpiece, dated 1693, and on either side two windows. On each floor at the front five large windows faced south-east. The top of the façade was completed by a stepped gablehead. Inside there were around 20 rooms consisting of large public rooms, extensive bed chambers, servants' quarters, kitchen and pantries.

Sir John Clerk was one of the most important landscape designers of his day. A man of exceptional talents and interest, he designed the landscape at Cammo, features of which still survive to this day.

Sir John's interests were extensive, politics, poetry, travelling, architecture and music to name a few. The importance of his work at Cammo must not be underestimated, as so often it is. This was possibly his first design undertaking, and as any gardener knows its always the one they learn from.

He undertook the planting and forming enclosures of fields between 1710-1722 he planted "several thousand trees" makes "sloaping bancks and the parterrs". He constructs "a summer house at the end of the great avenue" in 1714 and continues planting orchards and plantations.

In an era where more elaborate gardens of terraces, water features & clipped parterre were fashionable, Sir John goes towards a more naturalistic appearance, but this is also partly due to the relatively modest income he had in comparison to owners of larger, greater estates.

By 1722 he had become the 2nd Baronet of Penicuik and sold Cammo in 1724 as the majority of his land holdings were south of the Pentland hills and he took residence in Penicuik House.

In 1757 a new bridge was built across the River Almond beside what is now Craigiehall, the Army Headquarters for Scotland until 2015, at a cost of exactly £15.

The next major changes were carried out by Charles Watson, who inherited the house and estate on the death of his father. One of the first projects he carried out was to construct the east and west walls of the new garden in 1781 and then the north and south walls the following year. This garden is still here today and, although overgrown and wooded, it is still possible to locate the former lean-to potting sheds and hot walls and flues. These were used to cultivate delicate fruit such as peaches. The walls also contain 'bee boles' (bee hives which are located in a warm eastern wall) which could easily be accessed to harvest the honey, and a pair of tall banded and polished gatepieces with moulded bases at the entrance to the garden. (The bee boles are shown in a photograph at the end of this publication.)

In conjunction with these changes to the garden, major improvements were being made to the house. Builders' receipts show that between 1782 and 1783 a new dining room was completed and woodwork was put in place. The services of an upholsterer were called upon to 'canvas and hand paper in the room' at a cost of £25 19s, which also included work in the dining room. Also at this time the woodwork in the drawing room, dressing room and dining rooms were gilded, a rather expensive process costing £36 9s 9d.

It seems strange that it was cheaper to build a bridge which has lasted over 200 years than to gild woodwork and shelving, which was probably altered when fashions changed.

In 1789 a gate lodge was built at the end of the north-east entrance at a cost of £62. The structure is single storey with a three-bay window facing up the main drive. The entrance doorway has a single stone surround. A lintel over this shows the initials of Charles Watson and the date 1789 flanked by two rosettes.

To the left of the doorway is a gate pier adjoining the gatehouse. The end of the main gate pier is finished by iron railings. The four entrance gate piers are polished ashlar, each with a fluted frieze and moulded cornice with pyramidal caps finishing with a plain paid of iron gates weighing 666 lb and framed in the best manner which were cast at a price of £33 16s.

Estate papers from 1789 give details of wages relating to the staff. These are as follows:

A stable helper's salary was £7 10s on 13 November 1789. Presumably this was the annual salary for an experienced hand.

There were several manservants:

Robert Jackson	£6 19s
Peter Raeburn	£6 13s
William Liddle	£7 7s
Thomas Philip	£1 10s
Daniel Cameron	£1 10s

There were also two undergardeners:

Robert Turnbull	£1 10s
George Dickson	£1 10s

Meanwhile, work had already begun on the peron (an external stairway) and terrace, which was added to the front of the house around 1790. This consisted of a semicircular staircase and carved stone balustrade leading elegantly to the main entrance. The cost of this project was the huge sum of £300.

Once again, inside the house the services of an upholsterer were called upon. This time he was required to 'paper the housekeeper's room and paint the doors in rose' for a cost of £1 10s.

Outside in the garden, a greenhouse had been built against the outer east wall at a cost of £45.

"New Saughton, the seat of Charles Watson Esq. of Saughton".
An early engraving of Cammo House, 1794. HES

Charles Watson had a sundial brought to Cammo in 1795. This was believed to have come from Minto House in the Canongate. He had his name inscribed in the base. It consisted of a carved stone neoclassical shaft with a polyhedron dial. It was placed in the grounds to the west of the house.

In 1811, the stables to the north were constructed. They consisted of a U-plan classical, symmetrically built two-storey building. The central bay facing east supports an octagonal tower with a bullseye window and moulded surround to the front, and the ground floor was completed by tall windows to the loft. The surface of the ground was finished in setted cobbles surrounding the courtyard to the entrance. Most of these cobbles still remain reasonably intact.

In 1814 a north-west wing was added, which increased the size of Cammo considerably. Builders' receipts and papers from 1815 show that blinds were installed in the dining room. These were '2 venetian blinds measuring 9' 6" high by 4' 5" wide'. They cost £6 5s 3d on 7 July 1815.

A few weeks later, on 1 August 1815, Charles purchased the following from a leading glassware maker:

1 doz. finger cups	£1 11s 6d
1 doz. coolers	£1 11s 6d
2 doz. coines	£1 1s
1 pint decanter	£0 4s 6d
2 tumblers	£0 4s
4 bed tumblers	£0 4s

Charles also ordered a silver plate basket at £14, which would be placed in the dining room. It was probably around the middle of the nineteenth century that the Victorian gardens and flower beds were laid out. At this stage a balcony was added to the west side of the house. Later in the same century another balcony made of timber was added to the original south-west side of the house at the level of the second-floor windows which ran the length of the wall.

Looking towards the flower garden
on the south-west side, c.1890s. HES

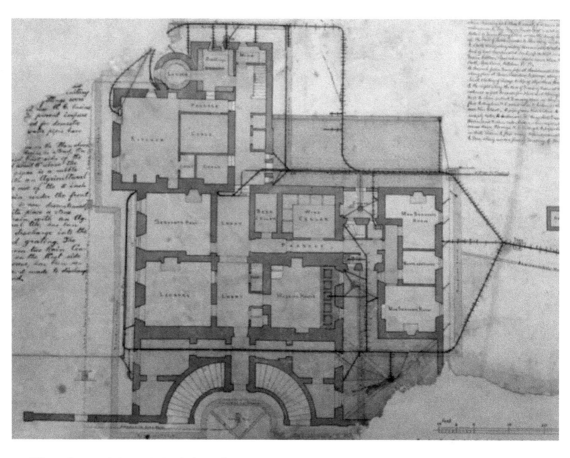

The only surviving original plan of Cammo. This shows the extensive basement and drainage layout. c.1890s. HES

The Maitland-Tennent Family

An exceptionally rare surviving family photo showing Margaret Louisa, her husband David Bennet Clark, Robert and a young Percival in the foreground. c.1900. SJB

Margaret Louisa Maitland-Tennent

Margaret Louisa Tennent was born in Edinburgh in 1859, her parents being Robert Tennent and Wilhelmina Meldrum from Kincaple. Her father had accumulated his fortune from sheep farming in Australia.

Her father also had extensive holdings and substantial property in the colony of Victoria, Australia.

Margaret had a sister called Charlotte Maud Tennent, who sadly died tragically at 23 Buckingham Terrace, Edinburgh on 5th August 1885, aged 24. The cause of this sudden death was "injury to the brain as a result of a fall from a window during sleep". This must have had a devastating effect on the family.

Margaret's father died at Kincaple House, St. Andrews (Kincaple had been built by his wife's family, the Meldrums, in 1789) in 1891, and his total estate was valued at £80,000 (equates to £7 million in 2017). Robert's wife Wilhelmina was left an annuity from the trust of £300 per annum (equates to £33,000 in 2017).

In 1914, just before the outbreak of WWI, her mother Wilhelmina died at Clunemore House, Drumnadrochit, Invernessshire. Coincidentally, this property is currently on the market in 2017 at offers over £390,000.

Wilhelmina's will stated her income from the trust set up by her father was to be left to Margaret and after her death, the capital to be left to her eldest son Robert. Sadly, this was never to happen.

After her mother's death, Margaret took her sons abroad, to avoid her eldest son Robert being called up for national service. The property valuation rolls for 1914 show Cammo House, Lodge & parks as vacant, and indeed the house etc was still listed as vacant in 1921. The only details were c/o contact details, being the Yokohama Bank, Japan.

By 1915 the family were recorded as sailing from Portsmouth en route to Wellington, New Zealand aboard the *Ruahine*. Margaret was aged 53, Robert 20, and Percival 14. While they were overseas their estranged father David Bennet Clark had died at his home in England.

It's not known what happened between his mother and his brother on this trip, but Robert refused to return home with them, and remained in the United States. Perhaps he could foresee his life taking a path he did not want to take, one which would have restrictions and a closed existence living at Cammo. On Margaret's return to Scotland with Percival, Robert was written out of her will. This action would cause great distress for Robert in future years.

Margaret was a sure headed and determined young lady who was very well educated and who went on to attend classes for young ladies at Edinburgh University from 1874 till 1881. In 1884 she became engaged to David Bennett Clark, who was a clerk with the Bank of Scotland. When they married three years later a contract was drawn up stating that he would never be entitled to the £80,000 fortune that Margaret would inherit one day. However, in 1900 they admitted that the marriage was not working out, and the next year David confessed his intention to take control, claim the fortune and dispose of it as he wished. By July 1901 he had been forgiven and returned to Cammo, but he had to pay his wife board and lodging amounting to 13 shillings per day.

In order to raise extra funds for investment and to maximise use of the land surrounding the estate, ground was leased to establish Cammo Golf Club in 1907, but on the condition that only Mrs Maitland-Tennent and her guests were permitted to play on a Sunday, when they would have the entire course to themselves.

Around 1910 she changed her name from Clark-Tennent to Maitland-Tennent, for reasons unknown. In 1910 she was divorced from her husband 'on the ground of desertion'. He moved to England and Margaret and her two children continued their life at Cammo.

In the 1930s the two remaining servants left Cammo and Percival and his mother were left to care for themselves. The servants certainly had the most up-to-date facilities. All rooms had wash-hand basins with hot and cold running water and polished granite floors.

In 1949 Mrs Maitlant-Tennent was once again involved in legal action, but this time as a defendant. She refused to reveal to the government the amount of funds held by her in banks in America and Canada. It was estimated to be around $117,282 (about £42,000 at that time). She was taken by the police and held in a cell overnight; when she still refused to reveal any information she was subsequently fined £50 by the Treasury. This was another example of her stubbornness.

When the tenant farmer, Neil Little, arrived in 1951 the stables contained two magnificent horse-drawn carriages from a past era. They were beginning to show signs of woodworm and rot, but their glorious hand-painted colour still remained.

Mrs Maitlant-Tennent died in 1955 aged 95, and was buried under the lawn to the west of the house. This was the last interment in private ground in Scotland. As a mark of his respect, Percival planted the area with daffodils, which were his mother's favourite flowers, and spent a considerable amount of money on floral tributes for the grave. After she died her estate was estimated to be £500,000, although it is thought that the death duties accounted for a large part of this sum.

David Bennet Clark

David Bennet Clark was born in Edinburgh in 1857 to William and Georgina Marjory Pearson (nee Dalziel) Bennet Clark, at 10 Manor Place.

He was one of three; his brothers were George and Thomas. George would go on to become a writer to the Signet, and married his wife Harriet in 1882 and lived at Douglas Crescent for 40 years. They had a son called Thomas Wilfred, who became a Captain in the 9th Royal Scots during WWI. When his father died, Thomas was living at 45 Moray Place. He died in 1963 aged 76.

David was a bank accountant at the Bank of Scotland, and married Margaret Louisa Tennent on the 3rd February 1887 at St. George's church, with his brother Thomas as a witness. Their first son Robert was born in 1892, and his brother Percival in 1898.

When David and Margaret got married a pre-nuptial agreement was drawn up stating that he would never be entitled to her substantial £80,000 fortune (about £4.7m in 2017). By 1900 there were problems within the marriage, and her husband admitted he had intended to seize Margaret and claim she was mentally incapable, thereby gaining access to her wealth.

Perhaps he had seen his wife's true character, and one wonders if he foresaw the troubles that would befall Cammo in the future?

By July of 1901, he had been forgiven by his wife and returned to live at Cammo, but had to agree to pay 13 shillings a day (£74) to Margaret for his board and lodging!

Clearly issues had not been resolved, as in 1910 they divorced on the grounds "of desertion by her husband" and David retreated to the south of England.

He passed away in 1923 aged 66. Who knows what secrets he kept with him about his family and his turbulent time with his wife Margaret Louisa Clark-Tennent?

Robert William Tennent

Robert was the eldest son and was born on the 17th May 1892 in the parish of Cramond, Edinburgh.

A relaxed Robert outside his home he built in Edgemont Street, Riverside, CA, May 1956. SJB

An extrovert, he was outgoing and intelligent and was a vegetarian who believed in alternative homeopathic medicine.

In 1915 aged 20, along with his brother, aged 14, he was taken by his mother Margaret to New Zealand. On the 2nd June 1915 they sailed from Plymouth onboard the *Ruahine*, a 6828-tonne registered passenger liner.

The timing of this trip was, I imagine, to prevent Robert being called for national service and if Percival was also out of the country, as war raged, in a few years he too would be spared the horrors of war.

After New Zealand they travelled to Australia (where their maternal grandparents had built up the family fortune) then onto Japan. Just how long they stayed in Japan is unclear, as between the years 1915 and 1921 the valuation rolls for property listed Cammo as 'vacant' with a contact address of c/o The Yokohama Bank, Japan.

Robert was clearly a very independently minded man, and he refused to return home with them as he 'refused to bury himself at Cammo' and live the secluded lifestyle his mother and brother wanted him to live, perhaps as a consequence of the dissolution of his parents' marriage. Letters many many years in the future confirm this.

By 1924 he had become a US citizen, and in the census of 1930, he was listed as a chauffeur living with Mr Frank B Clark and his wife Blanche, in a residence on Adelaide Drive (which still exists) in Santa Monica, CA.

Robert had achieved his wish and was living his life, away from the restrictions of his family.

Throughout the intervening years, he lived in Riverside, CA, and was employed in real estate and then the insurance industry. He built his own house (which is wonderfully described by an old neighbour).

> Edgemont is an unpretentious little town, situated along the main route crossing the State of California. Millions of people have driven by it, but no doubt, most without noting the name of the place, unless they needed gas, or a bite to eat, or because their cars overheated, coming uphill from Riverside.
>
> Though most of the houses are at some distance from the highway, there are times when the residents of Edgemont must plug their ears to keep out the roaring of jets from the military air base to the south, or the noise from the cars on the raceway to the east; and their eyes smart from the smog blowing in from the north and west.
>
> But on some mornings, as you go out your front door to bring in the newspaper, you linger a while, and look at the sky and mountains. The smell of blossoms is in the air, and the only noise you hear is the humming of insects and the cackling of a few chickens in somebody's back yard. Some of the newer houses around here look quite impressive. But the older, more modest ones have the luxury of big yards, some with carefully manicured lawns and hedges. But here and there you see a house surrounded by a half acre of desert, reminiscent of a time when building lots were sold by acres - not by square yards or feet as they are now!

In that town, there is one house that looks like no other house that you or I have ever seen. It's hidden away a bit. Likely it may have been here before the street was built that is close to it now. Some distance away from that street there is a large gate. Beyond it are trees, and a bit farther a small gate. Beyond that, the house is to your left. But to actually see it, you'd have to walk away some distance in another direction. Then you would see that the house has a second story, looking like another whole house, but smaller, built on top of the main house. It may remind you of a castle, with a look-out tower

-1-

-2-

on top. There is a patio next to the house, and on the other side of the patio a tiny fish pond, surrounded by a luxurious growth of plants. The builder, owner, and sole resident of this house is Mr. Robert Tennent, whom some people simply call "Bob". No doubt in his native Scotland he was addressed by a longer, more formal title. This and many other things he left behind more than half a century ago, in order to lead a life less restricted by conventions. But whatever he may have left behind, among the things that he brought with him and retained through all the ups and downs of a long and eventful life is a gentle and delightful sense of humor.

A.W.

(an old neighbor)

Even at Cammo he had been practical, as he installed a small generator to recharge the batteries for the cars. If there was something regarding the house construction he didn't know, he would go and observe how other homes were being built nearby.

In 1946 an action was raised in the US courts against his mother, for her failure to uphold a contract drawn up in 1914, which Robert was to be paid '£50 on Whitsunday and Martinmas each year', 'for love, favour and affection I have and bear my eldest son'. The payments were made up until 1934. The amount being sought was £1515 (approx £60,000 in 2017).

On the 3rd October 1951, Robert sailed from Quebec to Southampton for a stay of two months, presumably to visit his family, however in September 1953 he sailed from Glasgow to Montreal; perhaps at this point he was still trying to hold out an olive branch of reconciliation towards his mother and brother.

In 1955 his mother Margaret died and all assets were left to Percival, with no provision or bequest for Robert. This must have been an awful time: losing his mother, despite their differences, the trips back from the States to try and reconcile with them having come to nothing. During this time he would have seen how much his family home was deteriorating.

Once again the travel and immigration records show he left from New York to Southampton on the SS *America* in February 1959, for a visit of three months, staying with a Mrs G C Bonthorne, of 33 William Street, Kirkcaldy. The following year he had been in Scotland again, and this time, instead of sailing, he flew home from Prestwick to New York.

If Robert thought the disagreements with his mother had been distressing, more was to come when Percival died in 1975. He didn't attend his brother's funeral within the Dean Cemetery.

For the next few years, Robert was to be engaged in constant correspondence between his brother's executor Mr Lawrence Kerr, his own solicitor Mr Ian Ross, and the beneficiaries of Percival's estate, The National Trust for Scotland.

The letters between him and Mr Ross make for bleak reading, as he tried to retrieve property and items left to him by his grandmother in her will... mostly in vain.

Percival's lawyer Mr Kerr was incapable of dealing with such a complex estate. Eventually he did receive his christening silver, which comprised a milk pitcher and porringer, which had been a gift from the staff at Cammo in 1892.

Throughout all this time the press had been following events, and several articles about Robert appeared in print; this must have added to the emotional distress. His close family had all passed away, his family home in an increasingly perilous state, its interior neglected and damaged, family belongings strewn around.

Mr Ross successfully achieved a settlement in kind from Percival's estate. This was was £13,000 (approx £86,000 in 2017).

Robert never returned to Scotland, but he did continue to write to the Little family, who since the 1950s had been the tenant farmers at Cammo Home Farm.

At some point after 1978 there was a fire at Robert's home, and he was looked after by the American Red Cross for a while and a lady who lived close by. He lived in a motor home in her garden and each year went on holiday to Hawaii, but despite saying each year it was getting too busy and expensive, would return the following year. He remained very active and had a sharp mind.

On the 20th September 1986, Robert passed away aged 94 years and 3 months. He had never married, and his funeral was handled by close friends Mr and Mrs Anderson. He was interred in the Olivewood Memorial Park, Riverside, CA, a simple headstone marking his grave. Robert's estate was valued around $500,000 after his death. Monies were left to various charities.

In 2000 I paid a visit to Riverside, and found an empty site, surrounded by desert and the occasional other home. It was here I met Anne Marie Watson, a lovely elderly lady, who had lived opposite Robert.

She recalled his friendly, good humoured nature, very polite, helpful, but also that he never really divulged much about his previous life in Scotland.

Robert clearly had a privileged life, was well travelled, and in the States lived the life he wanted to live, but I doubt he ever really got over the awful way his family treated him.

Percival Louis Maitland-Tennent

Percival was born in Edinburgh on 8 November 1898. He was very intelligent and mostly self-taught. He liked to keep up with current affairs and was a keen follower of politics, which led to heated discussions in the household. He was, however, very self-conscious about his appearance because he had a severe curvature of the spine such that when he walked he always looked down to the ground.

While Mrs Maitland-Tennent was alive, Percival cared for and looked after his mother. He was a devoted son and would take her out in his black Humber car. They also had an old caravan from the 1930s and would often go touring round the highlands and west coast of Scotland.

Rumours regarding their lifestyle were rife. The Maitland-Tennents were *not* recluses. They went out every day for their shopping. They bought their bread form a shop at Bruntsfield and other groceries from shops in both Blackhall and Davidsons Mains. Ironmongery and dog food were purchased from a shop in Morrison Street and they went to Newhaven for fresh fish. They also went to visit the family lawyer once a week and were regular customers of Edinburgh's oldest department store, Jenners. Mrs Maitland-Tennent and Percival were shown into a private office when they arrived at the store and goods were brought to them so that they did not have to mix with the other customers.

The family were very well travelled. They visited Japan, Portugal, Hong Kong, Canada, San Francisco and elsewhere in America, sometimes staying away for weeks at a time.

Percival was very keen on cars. He always bought a car with cash and did not take out insurance; in fact, it is not known if he even had a driving licence! He would drive the car until it fell apart, then simply take it round to the back of the stables or into the woods and leave it to rust and decay. When the National Trust were exploring the grounds they discovered no fewer than six rusted car chassis lying near the stables. One of his other interests was monitoring the weather from a small station on part of the flat roof of the house. He first became interested after his grandfather taught him how to take readings from the barometers and precipitation devices.

Percival had another love: his dogs. Most of the dogs he had were animals that would otherwise have been put down. He could not bear to hear of any animals being destroyed and rescued them. He had approximately 30, and each one had its own bowl. Percival would have been upset to know that after his death most of his dogs had to be put down because they were wild and tried to attack members of the National Trust when they first visited the house after his death.

After his mother died, the dogs became the most important things in Percival's life. In the morning after his breakfast he would fill a couple of ten-gallon milk churns with water at the farmhouse and drive up to the house. He would open up a room and let the dogs outside for exercise and then feed them. After they had finished he put them back inside and let out another group from a different room. The process was repeated throughout the day until they had all been out. This was how Percy spent his time each and every day.

Between 1955 and 1975 he lived at the farmhouse located near the main gate. Percy did not live in a caravan as some newspapers reported at the time. He sat in the caravan and watched his dogs while they took their exercise. At the end of the day he returned to the farmhouse.

The farmhouse was home to the then tenant farmers, Mr and Mrs Little. Mrs Little cooked Percy's meals and looked after him. Her own family were not allowed into the kitchen until Percy had finished eating. Mrs Little's daughter-in-law, Nancy, told of one such occasion when her youngest son had sneaked into the kitchen to watch Percy eating. He crawled under the table and appeared at Percy's side and was most surprised to find that he actually had a face. The wee boy had never seen Percy's face when he saw him outside because of his curved spine. Percy simply looked down at the boy at his side, winked at him and carried on eating.

While living at the farmhouse Percy had his own room, and this was his own private space. Although he was a very private man, once he came to know the family he would often confide in them about how he felt. Life at the farmhouse revolved around Percy. A relative recalls numerous occasions when they could not go to bed until he came back from looking after his dogs: 'Sometimes we could not go to bed until he came back, often as late as 2a.m.!'

Percival died on the 2 November 1975, aged 76. He had gone up to the house as usual to see his dogs. The Littles became slightly concerned as they had not seen him since breakfast. Percival was found in the house. He had died peacefully with his dogs beside him.

The cause of death was 'congestive cardiac failure' combined with 'chronic bronchitis'. It was also noted on the death certificate that he had been showing early signs of senility. Percival was buried in the family plot in the Dean Cemetery a few days later. The funeral was attended by around 20 mourners, which included the family lawyer and tenants from the estate. His brother Robert did not attend but sent a wreath. There was a wreath from his tenants.

Percival Louis Maitland-Tennent's Will and Bequests

A rare photograph of Percival Maitland-Tennent and one of his dogs, c.1970s. SJB

Percival had drawn up his will in 1955, after his mother Margaret's death, and had appointed two Executors, Hugh Albert Constantine and Lawrence Kerr.

Lawrence Kerr became the sole solicitor in charge of winding up the estate, this is where problems started to arise for the beneficiaries.

It was a full month before Kerr notified the NTS that they had been bequeathed Cammo and made no apology for doing so, and later it was to transpire that the NTS, had considered reporting Kerr to the law society, because of the dreadful way he had managed the saga. He had delayed in obtaining tradesman to secure Cammo, thus allowing vandals and further thefts to occur. The timescale for winding up the entire estate had dragged on for a weary 22 months!

Robert clearly was furious about the way his brothers estate had been dealt with, as he so states in his letters to the trust.

In his will Percival had made three bequests:

1. For payment of all my debts and funeral expenses.

2. Mr Little, the present tenant farmer, to remain at Cammo Home Farm at the rent agreed for the last year previous to my death, and life rent for Mr Little and/or his two sons until they see fit to end the tenancy for whatever reasons beknown to them.

3. I bequeath the entire residue of my estate, investments and my dwelling of Cammo House, Cammo Road, to the National Trust for Scotland for them to restore, upkeep and maintain my said dwelling of Cammo together with adjoining garden and grounds as a private residence for as long as possible, for any party or parties as selected by the Trust to do as they see fit.

The monetary value of this bequest amounted to £170,702.49 (£1,693,369.00 in 2017). This was nowhere near the amount of money required for the restoration of the house. The sum needed was estimated to be three times as much.

Percival's brother, Robert, was not left anything, not even any personal family items. Any possessions Robert did have had been claimed by his mother and brother, who refused to return his personal items from his quarters at Cammo. Robert had been denied any claim years ago when he announced he was going to stay in America. This was the reason that Cammo had been allowed to crumble and decay.

Mrs Maitland-Tennent and Percival did not want Robert to get his hands on the house and estate, as he had threatened to sell off the house and develop the land for housing. That was the prime motive for writing Robert out of the will. Robert was however not the type of person to carve up the estate; if he had been able to inherit the estate and prove that Percival was not of sound mind, the house would most certainly still have been standing. Percival and his mother decided that they would set about getting the house into such an atrocious condition that, even if he did manage to gain possession of the house and grounds, they would be past saving and be of no monetary value. They eventually achieved their goal because, by the time of Percival's death, the house was in an extremely dangerous and sad state.

The National Trust eventually agreed to take on the conditions of Percy's will, but with a great deal of apprehension. They knew that the amount of money left to them would not be sufficient, and were not particularly interested.

A few days before the Trust visited the property for the first time, they received a letter from Mr Lawrence Kerr, Percival's lawyer. An extract follows:

It is only fair to forewarn you, however, that the house, having been home to over thirty dogs for over twenty years, is in an indescribable condition, both internally and externally, and is structurally dangerous. Please visit at your own risk.

A memo from the Trust to its staff advising that transport would be laid on to take the party of 14 was circulated around its office. The party were advised to take 'gumboots, an old coat, which will get dirty, and a torch'. The minibus left Charlotte Square at 8.30 a.m. What greeted the party on its arrival was an unimaginable mess. When they arrived at the main gate they had to leave the bus and walk up the drive, through thick mud which covered the ground in patches. Eventually they came to the top of the drive. There was a considerable amount of excitement and anticipation at what they might find.

Suddenly the house loomed into view. The massive stone façade looked creepy and eerie although it was daylight, and it was almost completely surrounded by undergrowth.

Then they entered, the first outside visitors for almost 40 years. They were met with absolute filth and squalor. The floor of the entrance hall was thick with dog excrement. Once magnificent carved gilded mirrors from floor to ceiling were now covered in thick cobwebs and layers of dust, and reflected the sad sight of decay. Lumps of plaster and cornice from the ceiling covered the floor, which was soaking wet from water which had been coming through the roof for years. Slowly they picked their way across the floor to the bottom of the staircase. In front of them sat two rotten sofas, their wooden frames the only part to have survived the damp and rot.

The once gracious and elegant public rooms were now packed with rotting rubbish and festering furniture. All over the house the stench of dog excrement and damp lingered in the air. The Trust could not believe the condition to which the house had been allowed to deteriorate. Wall after wall was covered in enormous paintings: landscapes, still life studies and portraits were all now covered in green mould and fungus. In the drawing room stood a grand piano, surrounded by empty cardboard boxes and the stuffing from furniture which had been ripped out by the dogs. The framework of fine Victorian furniture stood out from underneath rotting silk curtains.

On one occasion John Little and his brother Adam entered one room and moved some rubbish bags to clear some space, when suddenly a bag split and a torrent of crisp £5 notes fell out and gently rustled as they fell to the floor. The collection of notes came from a variety of banks: the Union Bank of Scotland, the British Linen Bank and the Clydesdale Bank. There were also several different amounts of notes from abroad, their face value now worthless. They stood in amazement at the scene that lay in front of them.

A few years later when John and Nancy Little were living in Selby they noticed a sign in the window of an antique shop which said they were prepared to pay £25 per old £5 note – the same type of note that had spilled on to the floor at Cammo!

All through the house, packed into every room, were rusting tin cans, piles of rotting old newspapers, empty cardboard boxes, piles of musty moth-eaten curtains. The Trust representatives went from room to room, pausing only briefly at doorways to glance in. Each room was like the last, fine furniture suffering from woodworm, china and glassware covered in thick grime. At all times they avoided touching anything because of the risk of disease. The carved wooden staircase with its balustrading was covered in wood-eating fungus and riddled with wet rot.

They decided to look upstairs and uneasily ascended, being careful to avoid standing on the rotten steps. Upstairs was no better than the rest of the house. Bedrooms complete with furniture had been left and bed linen had yellowed with age. Fireplaces, complete with original gates and surrounds, were now clogged with thick soot and dust which had come down the chimneys and built up over the years. In one bedroom stood, virtually intact and free from any rot, a huge four-poster bed with its original canopy and beside it a beautiful walnut chest of drawers.

In the once formal Victorian dining room the National Trust discovered several Italian paintings (one sold for over £7,000 in 1977 when it was auctioned). They were unceremoniously propped up against the wall and covered in plaster dust and dirt. Other paintings had fallen from the wall when part of the ceiling had collapsed, and had broken from their frames when they hit the floor. It resembled something from a bomb site.

The party found themselves walking across the room with the floor crunching beneath their feet as they stepped on the remains of a once magnificent chandelier which had fallen from the ceiling and smashed into thousands of pieces on impact. Several paintings had bullet holes in them, the result of vandals using them for target practice. They discovered the flat-bedded billiard table sticking through the ceiling of the room below. There was also a considerable problem with rats and mice, not to mention fleas.

One of the most unusual discoveries was a solid steel door which had been made to look like an ordinary panelled door. At this discovery all sorts of ideas went through the minds of the party as to what could be behind such a door. Eventually, by using brute force, the door was breached and an air of excitement descended as it slowly opened. They could not believe what they saw! There on several steel shelves were over 100 pairs of brand new denim dungarees! The party from the Trust gave an almost disappointed chuckle at the 'priceless' contents behind the three-inch-thick steel door.

Back in the basement hung silver-plated serving salvers which had been there for so long that they had corroded and rusted. Two large wooden tables, where food and sumptuous dinners would have been prepared, now stood covered in a layer of dust. The kitchen range was just a pile of rusting iron which had discharged its contents of soot all over the floor.

The National Trust members could not believe that anybody could possibly let this happen to a property just because of a family squabble and had no idea how they could possibly restore the house with the money that was available to them. To repair the roof alone would use up most of the money never mind any building repairs. They had another look around and went outside, glad to be able to inhale fresh air. While exploring they had been taking photographs to record the condition of the interior.

Once outside they walked around the grounds, going where they could and battling their way through the undergrowth. One of the discoveries, to the west of the house, was a carved stone sundial bearing the initials of Charles Watson, a previous owner, and on the base the date 1795. After being restored the sundial is believed to have been relocated to a National Trust property in Fife, at the end of 1994.

Among their other discoveries were the remains of several cars around the woods beside the stables. They lay in rusted heaps of twisted metal. The stables themselves were semi-derelict and without a roof. The stables were once home to seven horses and a blacksmith's forge. The family were considered to have one of the finest carriages in the district. Behind the stables were some farm cottages and a piggery and barn.

A short distance from the stables was the walled garden. This was very overgrown and the outer walls were crumbling, a testament that the family wanted as much of the estate as possible destroyed. The National Trust party could just pick out the outline of ruined greenhouses and potting sheds. One of the features of the garden that had survived was the bee boles in the eastern wall.

One of the many cars owned by the family, c.1912. NTS

A graveyard of cars near the walled garden. From left, Morris Minor, Austin, Ford Anglia. c.1975. NTS

Remains of the Hudson Super Six in the undergrowth, 1975. NTS

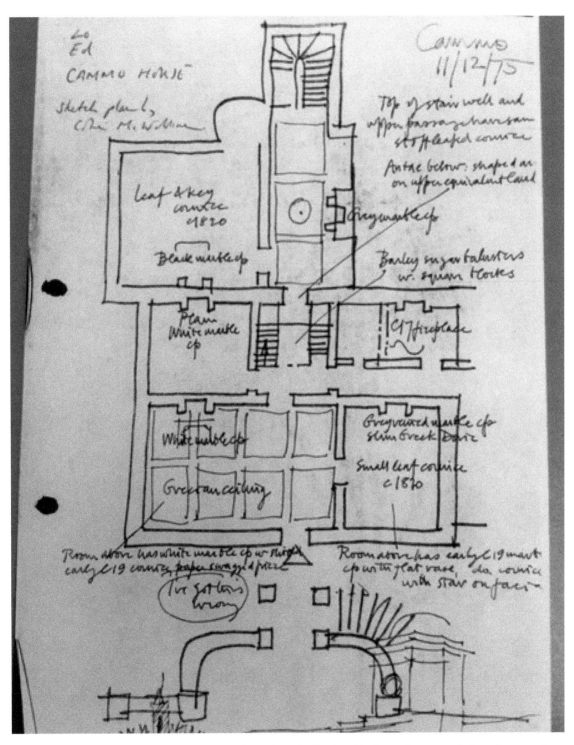

A sketch plan drawn by Chris Macwilliam dated 11/12/75. It shows the ground floor layout of reception rooms and fireplaces. NTS

The austere façade in 1975. NTS

The intrepid party from the National Trust for Scotland arriving for the first time in December 1975. NTS

The hallway looking towards the service stair, through the etched glass doors. The staircase was within the turret at the rear. The cobwebs are as impressive as the enormous gilt overmantel mirror. 1975. NTS

Abandoned food salvers hanging in the remains of the once bustling kitchen, 1975. NTS

A cellar room containing straw, 1975. NTS

The drawing room, its floor covered in dog faeces, 1975. NTS

A desk in the drawing room, 1975. NTS

The remains of a Victorian conversation seat. Its upholstery was destroyed by Percival Tennent's dogs. 1975. NTS

The sad condition of the dining room with its damaged Flemish and Italian school paintings, 1975. NTS

Ghostly view of the main staircase. The doorways shown lead to bedrooms at the front of Cammo. 1975. NTS

Various views of the staircase showing paintings in situ amid the damage caused by water, vermin and vandals. 1975. NTS

This illustrates the extent of dry rot affecting the house. Located on the landing it also shows the horrifying amount of dog faeces throughout Cammo. 1975. NTS

Damage in one of the upper bedrooms, caused by water penetration. Lead had been stolen from the roof on numerous occasions. 1975. NTS

A bedroom with the Victorian half tester bed in situ. 1975. NTS

An 18th century white marble fireplace sits amongst the rubbish of one of the bedrooms, 1975. NTS

Another view of the same room, 1975. NTS

The pipe organ was a treasured possession of Robert's. Sadly he never saw it returned to him. It was valued at £150 by the auction valuers in 1975. NTS

A large 18th century canvas hangs amid a damp-ridden staircase wall, 1975. NTS

The 18th century sundial brought from Minto House in the Canongate, Edinburgh by Charles Watson in 1795. It was originally positioned within the flower garden on the south west side of the house, where it was discovered in thick undergrowth in 1975. Now located within the visitor centre at the main entrance to Cammo. 2017. SJB

Detail of the damaged external staircase with its cast-iron balustrades, 1975. NTS

Detail of the garden balcony, 1975. NTS

Cammo boarded up in 1976. The wooden balcony was a 20th century addition. NTS

The entrance front showing James Johnston of the Scotsman newspaper, January 1976. JP

The rotten billiard table in the entrance hall, February 1976. DM

A grand piano smashed to pieces, February 1976. DM

A bedroom complete with Victorian half tester bed, February 1976. DM

This shows the kitchen in its heyday... complete with cook. Date unknown. NTS

Financial Dealings

When accountants, acting on behalf of lawyers, tried to unravel the family's finances, they discovered accounts in banks and investment schemes all around the world. Most of these accounts were known about, but there were a considerable number whose existence was previously unknown. These accounts were in America and Canada. In 1975, after Percy's death, the balance of these accounts amounted to a total of $31,674.94. This was held by the Bank of California in San Francisco. The sterling equivalent was £15,258.78. There had also, some 20 years earlier, been a balance of around $57,000 in Canadian banks. This had however been retrieved by the Inland Revenue to pay outstanding tax bills.

There were also accounts in Australia which amounted to $4560.25 (sterling equivalent £2803.64) and several in Japan, the sums involved being unclear.

The amounts held in British banks were also considerable. In the London branch of the Royal Bank of Scotland they held £2860.47, plus interest of £24.86. In the Edinburgh branch of the Bank of Scotland there were 12 separate receipt accounts each with a capital balance of £1,000. Most of these had been opened in the late fifties, and most of them had not had the interest added for many years! There were a further 15 accounts again each with a balance of £1,000 and again interest had not been added. The interest on all of these would be substantial.

The balance of all these accounts after Percival's death came to £170,702.49. This was made up of:

Heritable estate in Scotland £67,000.00
Moveable estate in Scotland . £100,817.16
Personal estate in England £2,885.33

After funeral expenses and debts had been cleared the residue of Percival's estate was left to the National Trust for Scotland. The Inland Revenue began to show interest in the estate as it realised that death duties, which it thought had been paid, had not.

There was some concern over the fact that rates had not been paid through the years. Mrs Maitland-Tennent did not believe in paying rates because the house had its own water supply and only had oil lamps throughout, so there was no need for any utilities. When it came to paying bills the family always paid in cash, even for large purchases such as cars. They never had any written contracts between tenants on the estate. Their word was their bond and they kept to it. They considered contracts and paperwork to be a waste of time.

Cramond Brig Golf Club

Cramond Brig Clubhouse c. 1912. SJB

The club was founded on the 12th March 1907, after Mrs Maitland-Tennent leased ground of approximately 54 acres on the right-hand side of the main drive. Mrs Maitland-Tennent was herself a keen golfer and was fortunate enough to have a course on her own estate. Not much is known about the layout of the course, although it was a full eighteen-hole course. In 1908, 350 members each paid four guineas' entrance fee and an annual subscription fee of £1 15s.

In 1909 a feu charter, in favour of the club, leased half an acre of ground for the building of a clubhouse. The clubhouse was built in 1910 to a design from 1908, by Bailey Scott Murphy and David Morton Kinross. It was an L: shaped A-symmetrical building in the Arts & Craft Style, with half timbering. The disposition contained strict guidelines on the construction and style of the clubhouse. The club was instructed to pay no less than £1,000 and when selecting iron railings these had to be of a design of Mrs Maitland-Tennent's choosing. In fact, such were the restrictions placed upon them, it is a wonder they were there at all. The text of the feu charter is given in the Appendix.

Mrs Maitland-Tennent banned members from playing golf on Sundays, so that she and her house guests could play at their leisure.

The Club, despite having over 700 members in the early twenties, fell into considerable rent arrears. In 1922 an Assignation was given to a director of the Club demanding immediate payment of the outstanding £500. The Club did not pay and Mrs Maitland-Tennent began to lose patience. She had previously been in dispute with the Club when she had planned to build a bigger wall around the estate. The wall, which was to pass in front of the Club's entrance, was never built after the Club adamantly refused to allow the construction.

As time passed the Club paid its outstanding debt but its leasing agreement was not renewed as Mrs Maitland-Tennent was rapidly losing interest. The Club, sensing the impending end of its time at Cammo, took the step of leasing ground at Dalmahoy.

In 1927, the course at Cammo came to an end with the Club moving to its new location and taking the turf from the greens with it as it would 'take' more quickly than sowing new ones!

On the 12th August 1931 the Club paid a further debt of £500 to Mrs Maitland-Tennent and declared its resignation from the property. The land was turned over to pasture and during the Second World War, when the house was being used by the Air Ministry, Mrs Maitland-Tennent and Percival lived in the old clubhouse.

In 1951 the clubhouse, which was now known as Cammo Home Farm, was given to the tenant farmer, Mr Neil Little. He came from the Braehead Mains nearby, and took over the running of the farm. The farm is still run by the same family who have now been there for over 40 years.

Within the last few years the occupiers of the Farmhouse & surrounding farm have vacated the building. Although it was occupied by the last farmer, it wasn't habitable for modern living.

Empty for several years it was boarded up and left. It was the subject of a planning application by Cala Homes who wanted to demolish the building which was granted a "C Listed Building status" in February 1997.

It has since been demolished as it was beyond repair and restoration. The vacant land is now a hive of activity as a new private house is currently under construction. The surrounding trees are subject to a preservation order.

The funds from the sale of the land have been ring fenced by Edinburgh District Council EDC and the NTS to provide funding for future projects to benefit the community use and ongoing future projects for the estate as a whole.

Site of the old golf clubhouse, where now in 2017,
a new home is being constructed

Cramond Brig Golf Club Feu Charter 1909

FEU CHARTER BY
MARGARET LOUISA MAITLAND-TENNENT
OR CLARK-TENNENT
TO CRAMOND BRIG GOLF CLUB LTD.
4th MARCH 1909.

Reserve the following rights:

FIRST
Reserving always to me and my heirs and successors the whole coal shale, fossils, fireclay, ironstone, freestone, limestone and other mines, metals and minerals within the bounds of the area of ground hereby disponed with full power to search for work, win and carry away the same, the working thereof being always conducted so that the surface of the said area of ground shall not be broken, and I and my foresaids being bounded to pay all the damages occasioned by such working, as the same shall be acclaimed by two arbiters, one to be chosen by each party or by an oversman to be named by the said arbiters before entering upon the reference in case of their differing opinion.

SECOND
My said disponees shall be bound and obliged within one year from the date of entry hereinafter mentioned to erect on the said area of ground and complete a house which shall be of the value of not less than One Thousand pounds, and that on such site according to such detailed plans and elevations and of such description and materials shall be approved of in writing by me previous to the commencement of building operations declaring that no other buildings than the said house together with all the necessary outbuildings including stable accommodation, greenkeeper's house and club makers shop, detailed plans and elevations of which shall be submitted to and be approved by me in writing previous to their erection on the feu unless the same shall be authorised by me or my foresaids.

THIRD

No alterations or external alterations without permission in writing or any erections on said area of ground and said area of ground be laid out in garden ground or grass or shrubbery and shall always be kept clean and tidy and free from nuisances that may be offensive to the amenity of the neighbourhood.

FOURTH

Shall be bound to fence the area of ground whenever it may be called upon by me or my foresaids to do, and shall do in the following manner: construct a north-east boundary wall of stone and lime with cope and iron railings to an approved design of me or by my forebears.

FIFTH

To undertake and maintain the whole buildings and boundary walls and railings in good and sufficient repairs of the foresaid value.

SIXTH

My said disponees shall not be at liberty at any time to use the buildings on the said piece of ground if they should cease to be used as a Golf Club house as aforementioned for the manufacture or sale of spirituous or excisable liquors or as a smithy, cake house, shop or factory of any description whatsoever or for any purpose except as a private residence without the consent in writing of me or my disponees have power to use the Golf Club house and shall only be open during golfing hours and the Golf Club house to be kept shut on Sundays.

SEVENTH

My said disponees shall be bound to insure the whole buildings on the feu with an established insurance office and to exhibit and retain receipts for the annual premiums for me or my foresaids, and in the event of fire my said disponees shall be bound to restore them to the value herein before specified within one such year and shall not be altered in any style or manner other than of that built.

EIGHTH

It is effectually provided and declared that it shall be in the power of me and my foresaids to re-purchase and re-acquire the ground and the whole buildings that may be erected at any time whatsoever may be beneficial to myself or foresaids and a maximum sum of Two Thousand pounds be fixed, and shall not be lawful or in the power of my said disponees to sell or dispose the said area of ground hereby feud or any part to any person or persons whatsoever until they have first made a written offer to me, and shall be allowed sixty days to accepted or declare any offers and if the foresaid carries out such autories, decrees and writs relating to all or any part of the said area of ground or buildings, otherwise such deeds and writs shall be void and nil and if my said disponees shall contravene or fail to observe and implement any of the burdens or conditions shall forfeit all right and interest in the said area of ground, buildings revert to me or my foresaids.

Stealing and Looting

For a number of years the house suffered greatly from stealing and looting. It started after the papers reported Mrs Maitland-Tennent's death in 1955. Press reports claimed the house was packed with 'priceless antiques', and for over 20 years people helped themselves to anything that caught their eye. Percival was not able to stop them coming in and did not turn his dogs on them fearing that his animals would be hurt. On several occasions Percy had disturbed people ransacking the house in their hunt for items of value, and one afternoon had even come across a man chipping out one of the enormous marble fireplaces. As if this was not brazen enough the man just ignored Percy when he shouted at him and carried on. Such was the lack of respect and sheer nerve of these people.

One morning a local resident out walking discovered Percy tied to a tree. He was cold and very distressed and had been there all night. He was then in his early seventies. Those responsible were nothing more than vicious, callous thugs.

The police were called to the house on numerous occasions and caught groups of thieves escaping through the west gate. Their hauls included binbags full of china plates and dishes from the enormous dinner service, antique French clocks, silver cutlery, gold rings set with rubies and diamonds, brooches and books from the extensive library, in fact anything they could carry. However, when caught the thieves usually threw the bags on the ground, smashing their contents instantly. The thieves did not care what happened to any of the items as long as they could get some money for them.

Percival appeared in court several times to identify the looters, who were punished, but he refused to take back items that had been used in evidence on the grounds that they had been 'soiled and touched by undesirables'. Nobody knows what happened to the possessions that were not returned to Percy.

Although the house was in a bad condition, vandals and thieves had also caused much damage. Drawers had been pulled out and their contents strewn on the floor; paintings had been removed form their frames and thrown across the room; panelled doors had been smashed; windows and furniture broken up; all this in the hunt for money and items of jewellery.

Outside thieves had stolen lead from the roof, allowing water to penetrate the house, and lead-lined sinks and large quantities of lead pipes had been stolen, all for the sake of a few pounds.

The house also suffered the indignity of being a target for souvenir hunters. A great many of the public came to 'have a look around' although the house was a private residence. Several items were rescued by members of the public, who were concerned about the way that the beneficiaries had handled the entire Cammo affair, and deposited with historical bodies to ensure their safekeeping. Indeed, the Royal Commission has several items that were given to it; items such as photographs of Cammo from the turn of the century, letters to Mrs Maitland-Tennent and an inventory of the contents of the house from 1897.

Sadly, it will never be known what items were spirited away by people as a souvenir from Cammo, home of the 'Black Widow', as Mrs Maitland-Tennent came to be known.

The Final Chapter

After the National Trust for Scotland had paid its first visit to Cammo in 1975 staff returned several times to check the house and to compile an inventory. They had, of course, to sift through the contents of the house and to list the furniture, paintings and porcelain which had survived the decline of their surroundings and the thieves. Many items were removed as carefully as possible and taken away. The Trust employed a removal firm to empty the house. The firm's employees were supplied with overalls, rubber gloves, wellington boots and face-masks because of the risk of infection. At the end of each day the removers were hosed down with a special chemical detergent and the overalls disposed of because the risk of disease was so great.

Paintings that had been hanging for years were carefully moved outside and loaded onto a tractor to be taken down to the farmhouse, where they were hosed down and stored inside for a few days before being put in storage. Items of furniture that had avoided dry rot and were in one piece were likewise cleaned and taken to the farmhouse. Once the majority of furniture had been removed, the real dirty work of disposing of the rubbish and the dog excrement that covered all the floors throughout the house began. One room to the rear of the building contained the decomposing remains of several dead dogs. Percival may have been an animal lover, but this discovery makes one wonder if he ever arranged to bury those of his pets that died!

Meanwhile the farmhouse was a hive of activity. The tractor was continuously in use bringing load after load from the house. Tables, chairs and sideboards were scrubbed to remove most of the grime and then left to dry before being taken inside and stored. One room in the farmhouse was crammed to the ceiling with furniture and boxes of glassware and china, including several bone china serving platters, ranging in length from two to four feet, each delicately hand painted and decorated in gold leaf. These had been part of the enormous dinner service, containing well over 100 pieces, that would have graced the table in the dining room. This service contained full coffee and tea sets, dinner, side and serving plates, soup tureens, cups which were also hand painted and enormous decorative pieces. There were large Japanese ginger jars, complete with dome lids, that were over four feet in height.

Once outside, each piece had to be carefully washed with disinfectant, at all times being very careful not to damage any of them. In the farmhouse the Littles could hardly move for furniture, which made it difficult to avoid bumping into anything. Nancy Little recalls that one painting took up the entire length of the hallway, which is by no means small, and depicted Christ sitting at the Last Supper.

Auction Sales

In 1977 the contents of Cammo were put up for auction by Dowells (which later became Phillips) between March & May. There were five sales held, which were well attended, by antique dealers, collectors and spectators alike, who were eager to see for themselves the furnishings and paintings of this once fine mansion.

An inventory produced by the auctioneers lists a substantial number of 18th century Italian & Flemish school paintings. These consisted of biblical scenes, landscapes and portraits.

One such painting was by Luca Giordano (1634-1705) who was a baroque painter and printmaker. His career spanned 70 years working in Naples, Rome, Venice, Florence and Spain, where he was the court painter to Charles II. Giordanos works are in galleries around the globe.

The painting which was at Cammo is described as "A biblical scene with figures and Christ in a landscape 89 × 115 cms" sadly it has not been possible to locate where this ended up, but it was valued at £500 in 1976 (approx £3,800 in 2017).

The extent of the collection shows the diverse taste and fashions of previous owners of Cammo, who when sold the house and estate, generally sold the contents too.

Given the conditions the paintings and furnishings had been in for a number of years, and the very poor state they were in didn't diminish the enthusiasm of bidders. One London based dealer bought ten large canvases.

In the Dining room at Cammo, there was a painting entitled "Christ and the Adulteress" which was based on the original by Rubens. From images this appears to have been in relatively good condition.

Other notable works sold were by Angelica Kauffmann, Helen Allingham, David Allen, Claude Lorraine and John Russell amongst others.

Further sales included, Silver & Jewellery and Furniture, a lot of which was described as having no value due to its dreadful condition.

Household furnishings and oddments	£7,595.00

Public Auction	
Furniture	£3,618.00
Paintings	£21,765.00
42 separate pictures	£270.00
3 pictures	£1.00
Flower jugs etc.	£5.50
Lamps and metal figurine	£200.00
Vases, jugs, etc.	£625.00
Additional household items	£980.00
Total	£35,059.50

Among other items sold were several rare and unusual clocks, which were cleaned and repaired by the Edinburgh firm of Hamilton & Inches. One clock in particular was so unusual that even this famous company had no idea of its origin or even its value.

Eager bidders at the painting sale at Phillips, Edinburgh, February 1977. JP

The painting of a fox by John Russell RA (1745–1806) being auctioned by Phillips in Edinburgh, February 1977. JP

A selection of furnishings being viewed at Phillips, Edinburgh, February 1977. JP

Mirrors removed from Cammo being viewed at Phillips, Edinburgh, February 1977. JP

Fire wrecks Cammo House

S. 23/3/77

Cammo House, the Edinburgh mansion, where once the legendary "Black Widow" was waited on by a team of servants, was early today a smouldering ruin after fire had raged through the upper two storeys and destroyed the roof and staircase.

The blaze was discovered shortly after 10.30 p.m. and flames leaping from the roof could be seen over a wide area.

Firemen were hampered in their efforts to reach the building by the poor state of the driveway — which was inches deep in mud — and by the fact that they had to use hacksaws to break a succession of padlocked gates before reaching the isolated building.

Assistant Firemaster Andrew Tait, who was in charge of operations, said that the fire was "very serious" and was proving difficult to get at because of the dilapidated state of the interior of the building.

The roof and the staircase had gone, but his men had managed with the use of short hoses and high pressure hoses to surround the fire.

Firemen bring the Cammo House blaze under control.

Press cutting from the Evening News in March 1977 reporting the first fire. JP

1977 and Proposed Developments

After the contents had been sold and funds raised, the National Trust then had to decide what was the best way to repair the crumbling house. The money bequeathed and raised from the sale of contents simply was not enough, and ways had to be found to make maximum use of the land, but also to keep to the conditions specified by Percival in his will. Several ideas and suggestions were put forward, and it was decided that if possible, land would be sold for residential development to raise funds badly needed by the Trust. They received offers from builders outlining the number of proposed houses and amounts they were prepared to pay. One offer was for 96 houses covering an area of 24.2 acres to the southernmost corner of the estate for a price of £295,000, a high price even for 1975. It was however going to be a problem obtaining planning permission, as the land would have to be re-zoned for residential development and also because it was in direct contravention of Percy's will. In addition to this, plans were drawn up for the demolition of the early and later nineteenth-century wings of the house and to subdivide the original part of Cammo House into 15 separate flats, complete with one garage per flat. The grounds nearest the house were to remain as private gardens for residents, and the remainder of the land to be used as playing fields and recreational ground.

Other proposals that were carefully considered were that Cammo House, Gate House, Home Farm, stables and outbuildings were all to be demolished. After this a leisure/sports complex was to be built which would incorporate a games hall for badminton, squash, snooker, basketball and volleyball on the side of Cammo House and set into the woods behind the demolished building. Further ideas for complete coverage of the land by houses were suggested, including a brand new golf course built on the side of the original course, which could be private or public. Along with zoning problems and the disapproval shown by existing residents they also had to consider the noise levels from the new runway at Edinburgh Airport, which was due to open on the 1 April 1976.

Arson

While various committees and trustees were holding meetings and talking everything over, the house was left to fend for itself. Emptied of most of its contents and its last remaining dignity, it soon became an ideal, if dangerous, hang-out for teenagers and children.

On the 24th March 1977 Cammo was once again in the news. On the previous day, late in the evening, smoke was seen rising into the sky from the house. The fire brigade were called and were quickly on the scene. The firemen suffered a few setbacks after the engine became stuck in thick mud that covered the surface of the driveway and finally made their way up to the house to find it engulfed in huge flames and thick smoke. The hoses were turned on and the fight began. The fire had been started deliberately by vandals. The firemen struggled for a considerable time before bringing the blaze under control and eventually it was extinguished. The fire had been started at the rear of the house in the cellar and had quickly spread unhindered, completely destroying the staircase and the roof. A few rooms that still contained odd items were now covered in a thick layer of soot and the smell of smoke hung in the air.

The entire rear of the house (built in the early eighteenth century) was totally destroyed. All the floors had been destroyed and charred timbers lay among the rubble from walls which had collapsed.

Members of the National Trust surveyed the extent of the damage and enlisted workmen to brick up the windows and doorways to prevent vandals causing any more damage. However, this was not to prove effective in stopping the vandals, who in May 1977 once again set fire to the remainder of the house. Again when they arrived firemen were hampered by dense undergrowth surrounding the house. The fire left a gutted shell. The interior structure was completely burnt out and only the chimney stacks stood surrounded by the remaining outside walls.

The members of the Cammo Committee, which was set up in conjunction with the Trust, had no idea what direction to take now. They were left with a shell of a house which had 'no significant or historical interest' and without the 'funds required for the necessary restoration'.

A fireman stands amongst the rubble in the basement of Cammo after the fire in March 1977. JP

The rear of the fire-damaged early 19th century wing, 1977. NTS

The sad state of the facade in 1977. NTS

Garden front, 1977. NTS

*The garden front, the shell of the house
supported by scaffolding. 1979. NTS*

*This rear view shows the original 17th century
house in the middle, with the later additional
wings and the east side during demolition. The
scale of the building can be seen perfectly here.
1977. NTS*

*Dramatic interior view during demolition 1978.
The panelling and shutters which can be seen are
the remains of the drawing room. NTS*

The stables constructed in 1811, 1980. NTS

*Detail of the original whitewashed cellars, 1980.
NTS*

*The corner of the garden front showing the join
between the original house and the early 19th
century wing. Note the curved stone corbal, this
is part of the original 'twin curvilinear gables'
of the 1693 house. 1979. NTS*

Demolition

Some weeks later a representative from Edinburgh District Council EDC received reports that children had been seen on a number of occasions playing in and around the ruins of the house. The Council sent its Director of Building Control, Mr Ron Cooper, to investigate. Mr Cooper confirmed the reports and observed that there were no warning signs posted informing the public of the dangers. He spotted several children climbing up the already dangerous stonework. He reported back to the Council and then turned up at Cammo the next day with a bulldozer and demolition team. They started work right away pulling down a part of the remaining building.

By pure chance a National Trust representative arrived on the scene and discovered Mr Cooper and his team hard at work. He asked them to explain exactly what they thought they were doing and demanded that they stop immediately. He ordered them off the property since Mr Cooper had been acting without the consent of the Trust. He was officially halted by a 'stay of execution' issued by the Court in favour of the Trust. Press reports told of the house being saved from demolition and made safe, but this was not to be. The early nineteenth and twentieth century additions were removed and the original part of the house itself left. It was to stay for two years as a gutted shell standing alone and grim against the overgrown grounds. It was estimated in February 1979 that the total cost of restoration was a staggering £450,000, however the National Trust was not able to raise such funds for Cammo and the fate of the remainder of the house was the subject of further discussion.

Eventually it was decided, after talks with Edinburgh District Council, that the Trust would gift the estate and the remains of the house in a feu charter. This was carried out and the token sum of 'one new penny' was paid to the

National Trust in exchange for the estate.

In 1980 the Edinburgh firm of architects, Simpson & Brown, drew up plans for the final demolition of the remaining structure. Their idea was to remove the existing walls down to the level of the first floor windows and entrance doorway, thus leaving a 'safe ruin' and a focal point in the grounds which would become a 'wilderness park' for the people of Edinburgh.

Not long afterwards the work was complete and the existing shape was finished. It has left what, in my opinion, can only be described as a pointless pile of stones. The remains in no way whatsoever show the massive scale of the house or help to illustrate the design of the building.

In 1980 Cammo Estate became the UK's first 'Wilderness Park' and was handed over to the public in an official ceremony involving representatives of the National Trust, the Lord Provost of Edinburgh, the local MP and local residents.

So Cammo has changed little since then, the grounds thankfully have been saved from housing estates, leisure complexes and industrial units. However, the grounds have been neglected and are still overgrown. Funds which were left for the estate's restoration have not been spent for that purpose. Since 1980 very little has changed.

The rubble from the demolition was used as infill, this was later grassed over. 1980. NTS

An atmospheric early morning image of the final stages of repointing the remaining stonework, 1980. NTS

The formal handover from the National Trust for Scotland to Edinburgh District Council, 1980. NTS

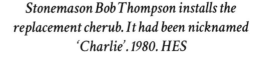

In 1980 the missing Cammo Cherub, which formed part of the 1693 door surround, was recarved, 1980. HES

Stonemason Bob Thompson installs the replacement cherub. It had been nicknamed 'Charlie'. 1980. HES

Robert William Maitland-Tennent's marker stone within Olivewood Memorial Park, Riverside, CA, 2017. SJB

The Cammo Crocodile found during the Edinburgh Archaeological Field Society's dig in July 2017. A very detailed heavy cast metal piece still showing traces of blue enamelling. EAFS

The Tennent family plot within the Dean Cemetery, Edinburgh. This is where Margaret Louisa was re-interred after being exhumed from the flower garden at Cammo. It's also the the resting place of her father Robert, her younger sister Charlotte, and Percival. 2017. SJB

The entrance gates with a posed figure, c.1896. NTS

The gate lodge built in 1789, being viewed by members from the National Trust for Scotland in 1976. NTS

Water tower in the 1950s. This is an iconic feature seen by drivers every day on the Maybury road. HES

The same building after restoration in the 1990s. 2017. SJB

Cammo House and Estate in 2017

Anyone who has visited Cammo for the first time can be left with a sense of confusion when viewing the remains of the "big house".

The current structure doesn't give an idea of the imposing scale of the house which had stood for nearly 285 years.

The entrance front which faces south east, has been reduced to the principal floor level and the stone window surrounds, have been halved in height. The 17th century carved stone doorway is the only remaining feature to have survived the bulldozers. The date of 1693 and the carved bearded face can still be seen.

A semi-circular entrance staircase which once greeted visitors to Cammo in its prime, had suffered from vandalism and was removed during the demolition. It has been replaced by a grassed slope with wooden sleeper steps which now lead up to the doorway. The grassed slope continues around both sides, gradually tapering down to ground level.

The "interior" of the house is now grassed over, rubble from the demolition being underneath.

Venturing further around the estate other structures and features have remained despite the ravages of time. The once busy stables with their ancillary offices, forge, tack room, piggery, cart sheds now derelict and quiet, their sounds of activity long forgotten in the past.

The walled garden, with its Vineries, Peach-house and conservatory, now sits with its tumbled down walls. The spring sees a profusion of snowdrops forming a carpet of white.

A statuesque stone castellated water tower stands proudly, near the "knoll" a landscape feature created by Sir John Clerk. The tower, originally supplying water to the house, is a local landmark for drivers along the Maybury Road.

Unfortunately the remaining grounds within the estate have not fared well with nearly a century of neglect. Regimented flower beds in the flower garden, next to the house, long gone and now under grass, but circles of daffodils appear to welcome spring. This was the original resting place of Margaret Louisa Tennent. Even now they remind us of the presence of the "black widow".

Amidst all this sits the Pinetum. A wonderful array of specimen trees. The ARANCARIA (monkey puzzle) almost 150 years old and originates from South America, is an excellent example of Victorian taste. A SEQUOIADENDRON GIGANTEU (Wellingtonia) around 152 years old, its soft red bark so tactile. Lost in the gales of 1994, was a stunning Lebanese Cedar, its gap now allowing other pines to flourish. One of the most unique trees at Cammo is SCIADOPITYS VERTICILLAT (the Japanese umbrella pine) around 140 years of age and which is recorded in the British Tree register as being the second largest in the UK. In the autumn the many mature Beech and Oak trees provide welcome colour.

The circumstances surrounding Cammos decline are truly unique.

Its downfall I feel truly started around 1910.

- The scandal of the divorce from her husband David Bennett Clerk.
- The world trip and the avoiding of either of her sons being called up for national service.
- The fallout between Margaret and her eldest son Robert.
- The actions of the US treasury for pursing Margaret for her illegal deposits of monies abroad.

At some point its as if she almost gave up on life, today it would be classed as a form of depression, which affects so many around the globe.

When Margaret died in 1955, the house having been empty for long periods of time and unmaintained, began a spiral of decay which ultimately would have only one outcome.

At the time of Percival's death in 1975, its days were over.

The lack of expediency by Lawrence Kerr, Percival's executor, in securing the property, in order to prevent further break-ins, thefts and vandalism further compounded Cammos fate.

The further lack of professionalism shown by Mr Kerr, in dealing with the administrative side.

The NationalTrust for Scotland were given a poisoned chalice from the offset.

The new regulations regarding Capital Transfer Tax (introduced in 1974 and replaced in 1986 by Inheritance Tax) were to be severe.

The provision of a sitting tenant on the estate, as a mark of gratitude from Percival.

An unrealistic amount of remaining capital to fund the requests by Percival.

Despite all that being said, I do feel that more should have been done.

More proposals for the development of the house should have been given more thought, whether in apartments or commercial use.

Even twenty-three years after writing the first version of The Private World of Cammo, I'm still distressed when I see the sheer waste and needless destruction, by the previous owners.

The needless loss of another part of Edinburghs heritage.

It could have been a fascinating time capsule of a Victorian & Edwardian family's life, their travels, interests and social history.

Now in the 21st century, over 40 years after Cammos destruction, we value our historic buildings more. We have organisations who can offer assistance & guidance for historic buildings, because if we don't value them they wont exist for future generations.

So the next time you visit Cammo, enjoy what you experience because it contains 1,300 years of history.

Simon Baillie
August 2017

The entrance lodge, 2017. SJB

Cammo House, 2017. SJB

The 18th century stone seat, once located in the flower garden, now at the entrance lodge, 2017. SJB

The original 17th century doorway, 2017. SJB

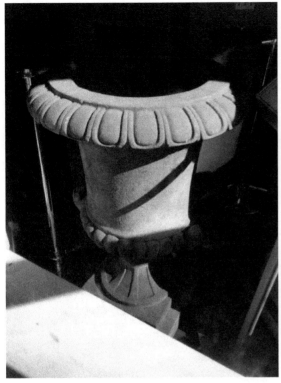 

One of a pair of stone urns which stood either side of the garden steps at the flower garden, 2017. SJB

One of the stone pineapple finials which were positioned on stone piers near the main entrance, 2017. SJB

 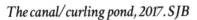 

The canal/curling pond, 2017. SJB

The flower garden, 2017. SJB

"Interior" showing the parlour windows to the left of the doorway, 2017. SJB

"Interior" showing the billiard room windows to the right of the entrance doorway. The fireplace opening and windows seen were in the basement servants' hall, 2017. SJB

The remains of the flue house with the vents which would have distributed the heat to warm the walls of the glasshouses, 2017. SJB

The entrance gates. These are replacements of the originals which were replaced for some unknown reason in the 1990s. 2017. SJB

Friends of Cammo

Registered Scottish Charity No. SC033394

FRIENDS OF CAMMO VISION FOR CAMMO ESTATE
"COUNTRY IN THE CITY"

INTRODUCTION

The purpose of this document is to set out a Vision for Cammo Estate that may then inform any future decisions on capital spending in the Estate.

In particular, the sale of Cammo Home Farm and a possible Heritage Lottery Fund bid present "a once in a generation" opportunity to invest in Cammo Estate in a way that can conserve and enhance its natural environment and built heritage, whilst making the landscape and visitor facilities more robust and fit for the future.

The need for a Vision for Cammo is also made more pressing by the fact that, in the near future, there may be over 3,000 new households within a mile of the Estate, with the possibility of developments including Maybury and West Craigs, Craigiehall and Cammo Fields. This will significantly increase the number of people using the Estate and may well degrade the Estate unless steps are taken to prepare it for heavier use.

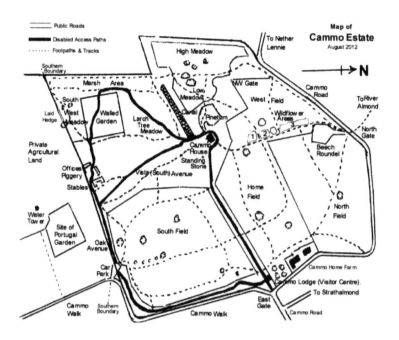

Cammo Estate is managed by City of Edinburgh Council as a public park, in accordance with a conservation agreement with the National Trust for Scotland.

THE VISION

This is our vision for Cammo Estate in 2030

Value to the Public

Cammo will be highly valued by the local community and visitors for its landscape, wildlife and historical values and for the opportunities it offers for low-key recreation, enjoyment and outdoor education. The Estate will continue to be appreciated because of the range of woodland, meadow and other habitats and countryside experiences it offers within a relatively small area and in close proximity to the city.

Extension of the Estate

The Estate will have been extended to reconnect with the historical features of Mauseley Hill, the Water Tower and site of the Portugal Garden.

Built Structures

The ruined Stables will have become a centre designed for activities related to education and conservation of the Estate. The Walled Garden will provide fruit for visitors and be a secluded haven. The walls and fences of the Estate will be safe and in good repair. The Canal will be attractive and clean and there will be a new water feature. Other historic features will be more prominent.

Landscape and Wildlife

The Estate will continue to consist of a mosaic of woodland, hedgerow and wildflower habitats providing high biodiversity value. Action will have been taken to ensure that this high biodiversity value is maintained or increased despite increased public use. Key elements of the historic landscape (e.g. avenues of trees) will have been conserved and strengthened.

Public Access, Orientation and Interpretation

Cammo will cater for the needs and interests of a broad visitor base, including young people and less able members of the community. There will be a well-maintained path network, good visitor facilities and increased parking. The Estate will form part of West Edinburgh's green networks of multi-use paths and wildlife corridors, such as the River Almond Walkway. High quality orientation, using signs and other media, will guide visitors around the Estate. Interpretation of key features will enhance visitors' awareness and appreciation of the Estate's wildlife, landscape and social history.

Education, Community Engagement, Volunteering and Sustainable Management

Cammo will have become a centre for education and training, based on its good quality, varied natural habitats. Cammo will be used by the local and wider community for guided walks and other events. Friends of Cammo, members of the local community and other volunteers are actively involved alongside the City Council and the National Trust for Scotland in the management of the Estate and development and implementation of a far-sighted, long-term management strategy.

> "In ten/twenty years' time, when Cammo is largely surrounded by new housing, it is hoped that Cammo will still be a little bit of 'Rus In Urbe' (Country in the City) and that children will be able to enjoy the simple pleasures of climbing trees, looking for certain flora and fauna, and running about in woodlands and fields, while their parents are able to enjoy the peace, quiet, stillness and birdsong of countryside."
>
> *Harry Taylor*
> *a long-time Friend of Cammo*

ACHIEVING THE VISION

Funding

A capital sum of around £400,000, ring-fenced for Cammo, will be received by City of Edinburgh Council in 2016 from the sale of Cammo Home Farm. This alone would enable many improvements to be made at Cammo. Additional funds would be required to achieve the full extent of this Vision, including restoration of the Walled Garden and Stables. City of Edinburgh Council intend to develop a Heritage Lottery Fund (HLF) bid for this, following their successful HLF bid for Saughton Park.

Development Pressures

The Local Development Plan (LDP) for Edinburgh identifies West Edinburgh as a strategic development area for additional housing. The LDP recognises that Cammo Estate and the neighbouring land including Mauseley Hill should not be developed, but recommends areas for housing at Maybury/West Craigs with up to 2000 units and the Cammo Fields next to Maybury Road with up to 700 units. These proposed developments in the green belt, particularly Cammo Fields, have met considerable opposition, and alternative locations may be favoured when the LDP is finalised. However there are new proposals for housing developments in the area going beyond the LDP, including up to 1200 units in a new Craigiehall Village centred on the army base, and increasing the housing capacity of the

International Business Gateway east of the airport to over 2000 units. Taken together, these potential developments will greatly increase the number of local residents for whom Cammo Estate will be an attractive green space.

Extension of the Estate

Extend the Estate to include the Water Tower, Mauseley Hill and the site of the Portugal Garden, which were historically parts of the estate. The additional area should be managed in a similar way to the rest of the Estate. This will:

- provide better access to these historical features from the rest of the Estate;
- enable the features to be safeguarded, conserved and managed in accordance with the strategy/plans for the Estate;
- absorb some of the additional visitors expected from nearby developments;
- reduce conflicts between visitors and agricultural use.

Built Features

Establish a longer-term plan and programme to reinstate (as required), enhance, conserve, manage and interpret the key historic features of the Estate, and increase their contribution to other objectives.

a) Ensure that all built features, including particularly the Walled Garden, Stables, other ruins, walls and fences are, as a minimum, safe to prevent injury to visitors and without Heras fencing that detracts from the historic feature.

b) Walled Garden:
- Expand the area of Scottish fruit, adding to the 2015 planting of apples, pears and plums to include raspberries, blackcurrants, blackberries, gooseberries etc. Visitors should be free to pick these and the Friends of Cammo to make jams and other products to sell.
- Create a Sensory Garden with quiet and sheltered seating areas.
- Provide an area for use as a seedling nursery, in which groups of children could propagate trees and bushes for later planting elsewhere at Cammo.

- Within the total area of 2.5 acres (1 hectare) maintain significant areas of native plants and trees including snowdrops amenity value. There should be no introduction of allotments and no formal planting.

c) Look at the potential for restoring the Stables in order to use it as a classroom/laboratory/studio/educational, arts and nature centre.

d) Ensure that the Canal is kept relatively clean and flowing without excessive organic build-up that leads to impoverishment of its biodiversity and amenity value.

e) Convert the Water Trough at the bottom of South Field into a water feature with sheltered seating and a wheelchair accessible path from the Lodge.

f) Clear the Golf Tee at the north-west corner of the Estate to bring out this feature of the early twentieth century golf course in order to illustrate an aspect of the changing land use and provide a new view point.

g) If the Estate is to be extended, assess the conservation and maintenance requirements for the Water Tower and ensure these are adequately funded. Enhance access to the Water Tower and to Mauseley Hill.

h) Create a modest-scale outdoor events area with natural seating (e.g. an outdoor auditorium with seating on grass slopes).

Landscape Features

a) Maintain and undertake new planting to strengthen the historic tree avenues: East Avenue from Lodge Gate to Cammo House, Vista (south) Avenue from House past Stables, Oak Avenue from Car Park to Stables.

b) Continue to offer the Pinetum as a location for new planting of exotic conifers, through the Botanic Garden's programme for endangered conifers and for other appropriate planting.

c) Where appropriate, plant native species and assist natural regeneration, to maintain mixed-aged woodland and consolidate woodland fragments.

d) Increase the protection of veteran trees and make more of a feature of them.

e) Create additional hedgerows, both following historic lines of the estate and, where appropriate, following paths and desire lines, including screening the Home Farm development.

f) Create additional wildflower areas, following the good practice developed at Cammo since 2011.

g) Seek to have wildflowers established in other large, grassy areas and manage the fields as wildflower meadows.

Wildlife

a) Ensure that the Estate is a Local Nature Reserve (LNR).
b) Adopt, as a fundamental policy of the Estate, the tenet that the habitat it provides for flora and fauna is central to its value. This is both because of the pressing need to keep an area of enhanced biodiversity close to an increasingly large urban centre, but also because, in so doing, we increase the amenity and educational value of the Estate to its users.
c) Increase the areas of the Estate that are under the three most valuable habitats in terms of biodiversity: the mixed-age woodland; the hedgerows; and the wildflower banks and meadows.
d) Create a wetland and boardwalk complex in South Field using the outflow from the canal. Open up this outflow from its current piped condition to an open stream.

Access and Enjoyment by All

Promote accessibility for all, including less able members of the community and families with young children.

a) Paths:
- Ensure that an appropriate network and mix of paths is established and maintained, some suitable for wheelchairs and pushchairs and some more natural.
- Expand the number of surfaced paths so that all visitors can see the main features of the Estate. To include new surfaced paths between Cammo House and North Gate to provide access from that gate, along the west side of the Estate to allow a full circuit of the estate, and along the north side of Home Field and back to the Lodge to provide a short loop for viewing wildflowers.
- Ensure that all paths are maintained in reasonable condition and that those designed to be suitable for wheelchairs and pushchairs are maintained in suitable condition for this use.

- Where possible, improve path design to reduce problems such as waterlogging, vegetation creep and erosion. Ensure that path construction is tree-friendly to prevent root damage.
- Install handrails and additional seating, in keeping with the natural environment, where this would be of most benefit to visitors.

b) Improve parking:
- Increase the amount of parking available on-site to cope with increased visitor numbers and reduce on-street parking. The least disruptive option on-site would be to expand the current car park into the corner of South Field. A hedgerow to surround the new car park would mitigate the visual and biodiversity impacts.
- Provide designated disabled parking.

c) Improve on-site visitor facilities:
- Visitor facilities are open for much longer than the current Lodge opening hours.
- Facilities at the Lodge and possibly also at a new Stables development.
- To include toilets (including disabled toilets) open at the main visiting times.
- Lodge to provide a welcoming entrance facility for the estate, information about the Estate, indoor exhibits and interpretation.

d) Promote suitable walking and cycling routes to Cammo Estate and management of these paths from current residential areas, new housing developments and the wider path network.
- Promote links with the River Almond Walkway, including its potential extension upstream beyond Grotto Bridge.
- Press for traffic free routes to be included in the Local Development Plan and planning applications.

e) Provide a cycle rack at the Lodge to encourage access by cycle rather than car, and to give these visitors the option of walking rather than cycling within the estate.

Orientation and Interpretation

Provide orientation and interpretation of key features, on-site and online.

f) Ensure that there are sufficient orientation and way-markers on-site for visitors to find their way to key features of the Estate.

g) Provide interpretation panels at key features, to help visitors better appreciate these features. Includes the Pinetum, Wildflower areas, Hedgerows, Cammo House and other features such as the Canal, Stables, Water Tower, Walled Garden and Veteran Trees.

h) Provide information and interpretation through digital media such as QR codes and apps, to enable additional features to be highlighted to users of these apps without the cost and potential clutter of excess panels, and to allow the information to be more easily updated.

i) Establish and maintain a website to provide more extensive information about Cammo Estate, to complement the current Facebook page.

j) Develop an improved map showing the layout of the Estate and the main features, and make it available in a free leaflet and online.

Education

a) Promote the use of the Estate by schools taking children out of the classroom to learn from nature including the sorts of activities provided through "Forest Schools".

b) Encourage the use of the Estate by youth groups such as Scouts, Girl Guides etc.

c) Encourage involvement in wildlife research and monitoring through relationships with local universities and interest groups.

d) Provide an indoor centre where groups can work on material collected in the Estate (for example in the Stables Block).

e) Provide facilities for younger visitors for natural play rather than a formal play area.

Community Engagement and Volunteering

Community:

Encourage the use of Cammo Estate for activities by the local and wider community:

a) Continue with the annual Friends of Cammo barbecue, bringing more of the local community, especially families, into Cammo Estate.
b) Enable the green in front of Cammo House to act as an arena to host additional arts and cultural events, e.g. a summer musical evening.
c) Provide illustrated talks at the Lodge or elsewhere, to entertain and inform about topics related to Cammo (e.g. bees, wildflowers, wildlife).
d) Organise and facilitate guided walks for particular groups including natural history and school groups and themed guided walks centred on biodiversity or historical features.
e) Promote the suitability of Cammo for health walks by organised groups.
f) Maintain the facilities for orienteering events encouraging community participation.
g) Promote collaboration between the Natural Heritage Service and community groups to put on joint events.

Volunteering:
a) Continue with Friends of Cammo volunteer activities including tree and hedgerow planting, wildflower area creation and maintenance, litter picking, Lodge opening etc and seek greater participation from members to increase these activities.
b) Encourage the use of Cammo for volunteer activities by other supervised groups.
c) Train some volunteers to undertake a wider range of duties (conservation work, patrolling and giving advice) as "Voluntary Rangers" under Friends of Cammo and City of Edinburgh Council auspices.

Educational and Training Programmes:
Develop training facilities and programmes, for example, training in conservation, woodcrafts and orchard management for special needs groups and schools, possibly with the Stables as a base.

Sustainable Management

a) Develop a far-sighted, long-term management strategy, supported by appropriate management plans and annual work plans.

b) The Friends of Cammo and other community groups should continue to actively represent community and user interests at regular meetings with representatives of the City Council and National Trust for Scotland in respect of their management and guardianship roles.

c) The City Council should continue to provide adequate financial and staff resources, supported by the Friends of Cammo and other volunteers, to ensure effective management of the Estate.

d) The Council and other funding sources should support conservation and development projects which are consistent with the agreed Vision and Management Plan.

e) The Local Development Plan and sensitive planning of surrounding areas should continue to provide robust and long-term protection of Cammo Estate's special values, i.e. its LNR status, overall biodiversity benefits and designed landscape, and also its wider setting, e.g. views to Mauseley Hill.

Friends of Cammo
June 2016

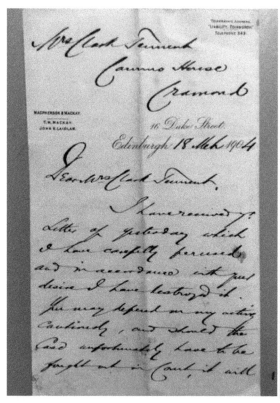

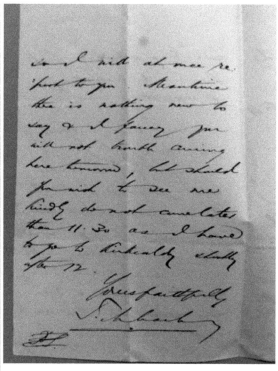

Lawyer's letter to Mrs Clark-Tennent, dated 1904. SJB

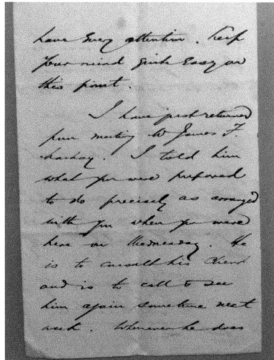

SS Tayio Maru, the passenger liner on which Robert sailed from Kobe, Japan, in 1925 to start a new life in the US.

15197 Edgemont Street,
Riverside, Calif. 92508

Nov. 25th 1977

The Director,
The National Trust for Scotland, Edinburgh, Scotland.

Dear Sir:

CAMMO

    I am Robert William Maitland Tennent, elder Brother of deceased
Percival Louis Maitland Tennent.

    Inasmuch as Mr. P.L.M.Tennent was deeply disturbed at my refusal
to adopt his mode of life of a recluse, he willed his estate of Cammo to
the National Trust for Scotland. This I believe he had the right to do.

    Unhappily, however in view of my refusal to conform to his
life style. Mr. Tennent absolutely refused to turn over to me my personal
property in the mansion house of Cammo. And he allowed all of this to
be subject to the destruction of the elements and theft with the exception
of several small items to which I will refer to later in this letter.

    In efforts to regain my personal property I made five trips from
America to Scotland, and though I talked with Mr. Tennent amicably he would not
give me any of my property nor did he even invite me into the Mansion House.

    Last February what was salvagable of the contents of Cammo
sold by auction. I would very much have liked to bid on some of
the items, and paid for them as they not my personal property. However
the sales were over before I received the auction catalogues.

    What deeply distressed me was the needless destruction by rain
and rot of my beautiful Bluthner Grand Piano. It was listed as of "no value"
I would dearly have loved to have had even the damaged remains.

    Saved from the sales were my silver milk pitched and porringer
which are silver and were among the silver belonging to my Brother. These
were given to me by the Staff at Cammo when I was christened and are inscribed with my name. As you can imagine these are of small cash value but
very great sentimental value to me Also and of small value were a few rings
which with the silver mugs Mr. Kerr verbally agreed to send me on settlement
of my claim which has now been effected. As he has not yet done so and there
is no reason why he should not as he is an honest gentleman I believe they
must be in the Trust's possession. Mr. Ian D. Ross of Messrs Thompson

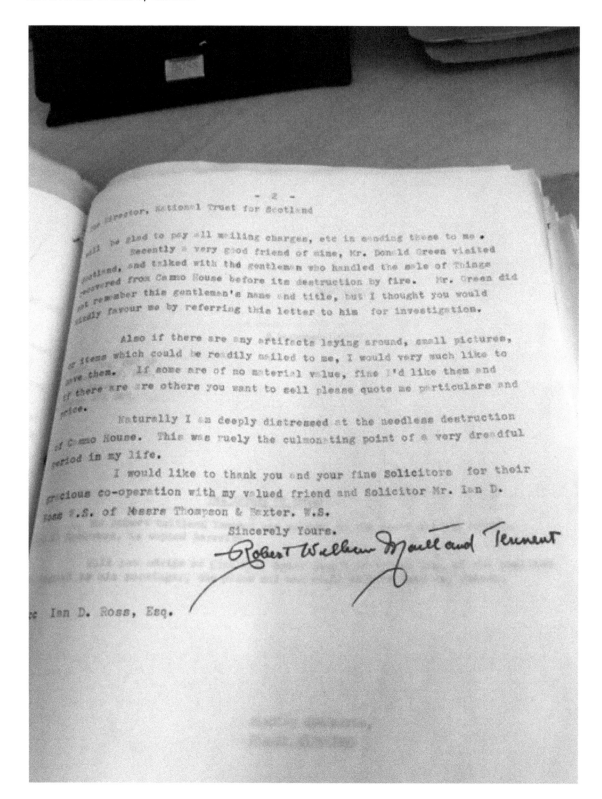

Riverside, Calif.   Feb. 15th 1977

Dear Mr. Little:-

I presume the sale of effects at Cammo including the jewelry silverware and pictures took place yesterday in Edinburgh.

Mr. Ross was able to rescue my silver mug and bowl from the items.   These items however contain manyof my PERSONAL property not coveredby items bequeathed to me in my beloved Grandmother's Wi.l.   Mr. Kerr took a long time to get in touch with Mr. Ross so I had no time to claim for items which clearly belong to me and which must now be gone for ever.

You will remember that soon after my brother died you turned over to Mr. Kerr some 16 rings and Mr. Kerr told you he would see I got some of these. He has never done so and I presume these items which include personal rings which belonged to me and were not part of my Grandmother's Estate which Mr. Kerr claims he has already paid for.

I am wondering if you were able to salvage any of my own books or small brig a brac.   I had a library of overv 200 books plus an upright Piano, Organ furniture etc etc in my quarters at Cammo, and which I asked my Brother time and again to turn over to me as they were my own personal property and had nothing to do with my Grandmother's Will, As you well know he absolutely refused to do so and they all became lost stolen or rendered worthless by the ravages of damp.

About all I can do now is to file a claim against my Brother's Will for the VALUE of my own personal effects, and have asked Mr. Ross to do this.   I would like to know how much the sale brought.   I believe the furniture and pictures should have been sold, but not the Jewelry and silver which cost comparatively little to store.

When you get a chance perhaps you will remind Mr. Kerr about the rigks you turned over to him. .

Naturally I feel very bad about the sale of the jewelry and silver which contained many items which were my own personal property so wrongfully misappropeiated by my mother and brother.   Any suggestions you may care to give me I will very carefully consider.

Hoping this finds you well and that the winter is not being too hard on you   Very sincerely

107

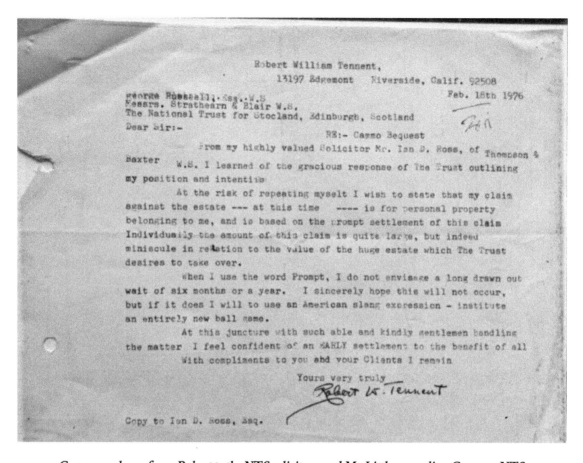

Robert William Tennent,
13197 Edgemont   Riverside, Calif. 92508

George Russell, Esq..W.S
Messrs. Strathearn & Blair W.S,
The National Trust for Scotland, Edinburgh, Scotland

Feb. 18th 1976

Dear Sir:-

RE:- Cammo Bequest

From my highly valued Solicitor Mr. Ian D. Ross, of Thompson & Baxter W.S. I learned of the gracious response of The Trust outlining my position and intention

At the risk of repeating myself I wish to state that my claim against the estate --- at this time   ---- is for personal property belonging to me, and is based on the prompt settlement of this claim Individually the amount of this claim is quite large, but indeed miniscule in relation to the value of the huge estate which The Trust desires to take over.

When I use the word Prompt, I do not envisage a long drawn out wait of six months or a year. I sincerely hope this will not occur, but if it does I will to use an American slang expression - institute an entirely new ball game.

At this juncture with such able and kindly gentlemen handling the matter I feel confident of an EARLY settlement to the benefit of all

With compliments to you and your Clients I remain

Yours very truly

Robert W. Tennent

Copy to Ian D. Ross, Esq.

Correspondence from Robert to the NTS solicitors and Mr Little regarding Cammo. NTS

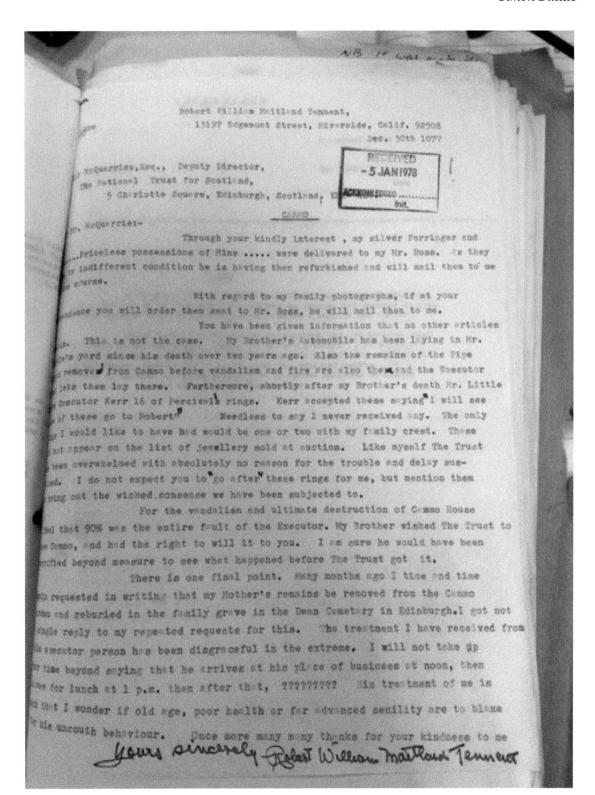

Robert William Maitland Tennent,
13197 Edgemont Street, Riverside, Calif. 92508
Dec. 30th 1977

RECEIVED
– 5 JAN 1978
ACKNOWLEDGED ....
Init.

McQuarries,Esq., Deputy Director,
The National Trust for Scotland,
5 Charlotte Square, Edinburgh, Scotland,

CAMMO

Mr. McQuarries:—

Through your kindly interest , my silver Porringer and Priceless possessions of Mine ..... were delivered to my Mr. Ross. As they indifferent condition he is having them refurbished and will mail them to me course.

With regard to my family photographs, if at your you will order them sent to Mr. Ross, he will mail them to me.

You have been given information that no other articles This is not the case. My Brother's Automobile has been laying in Mr. yard since his death over two years ago. Also the remains of the Pipe removed from Cammo before vandalism and fire are also them and the Executor lets them lay there. Furthermore, shortly after my Brother's death Mr. Little Executor Kerr 16 of Percivall rings. Kerr accepted these saying "I will see these go to Robert" Needless to say I never received any. The only I would like to have had would be one or two with my family crest. These not appear on the list of jewellery sold at auction. Like myself The Trust been overwhelmed with absolutely no reason for the trouble and delay sus— I do not expect you to "go after" these rings for me, but mention them ring out the wicked.nonsense we have been subjected to.

For the vandalism and ultimate destruction of Cammo House that 90% was the entire fault of the Executor. My Brother wished The Trust to Cammo, and had the right to will it to you. I am sure he would have been fied beyond measure to see what happened before The Trust got it.

There is one final point. Many months ago I time and time requested in writing that my Mother's remains be removed from the Cammo and reburied in the family grave in the Dean Cemetary in Edinburgh.I got not reply to my repeated requests for this. The treatment I have received from executor person has been disgraceful in the extreme. I will not take up time beyond saying that he arrives at his place of business at noon, then for lunch at 1 p.m. then after that, ????????? His treatment of me is that I wonder if old age, poor health or far advanced senility are to blame uncouth behaviour. Once more many many thanks for your kindness to me

Yours sincerely Robert William Maitland Tennent

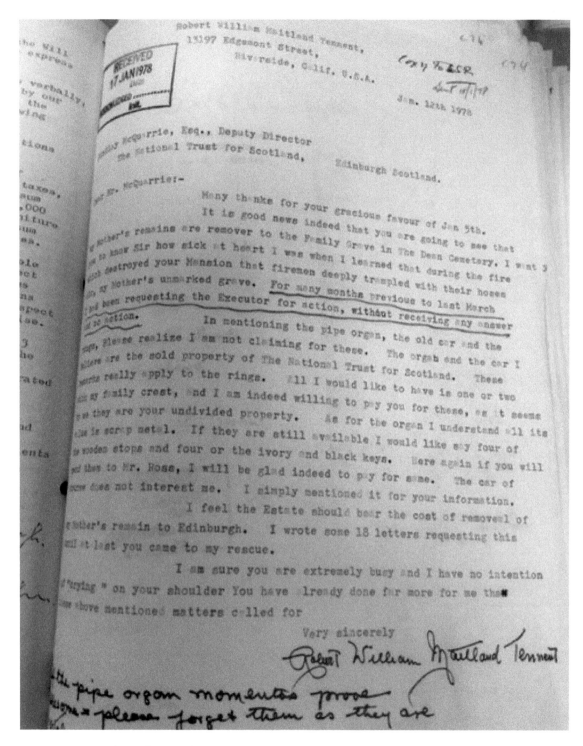

Correspondence from Robert to the NTS solicitors and Mr Little regarding Cammo. NTS

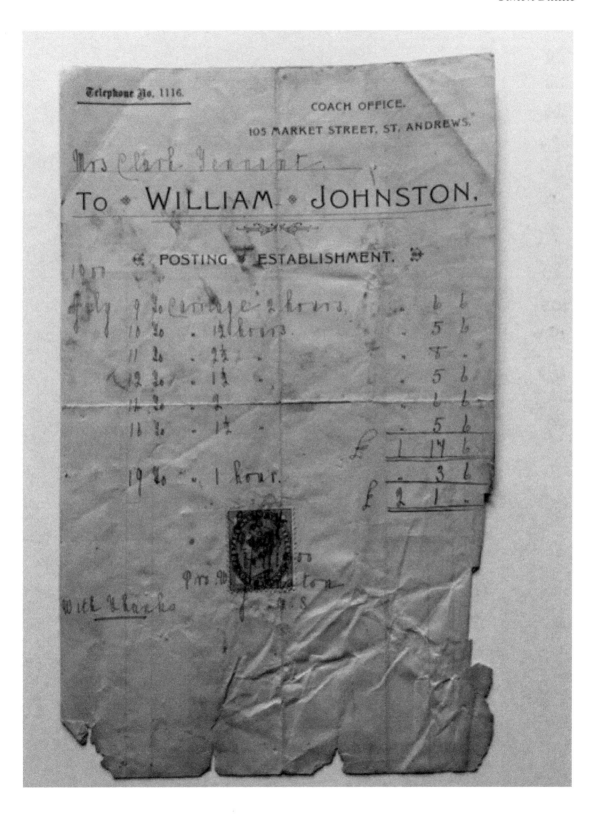

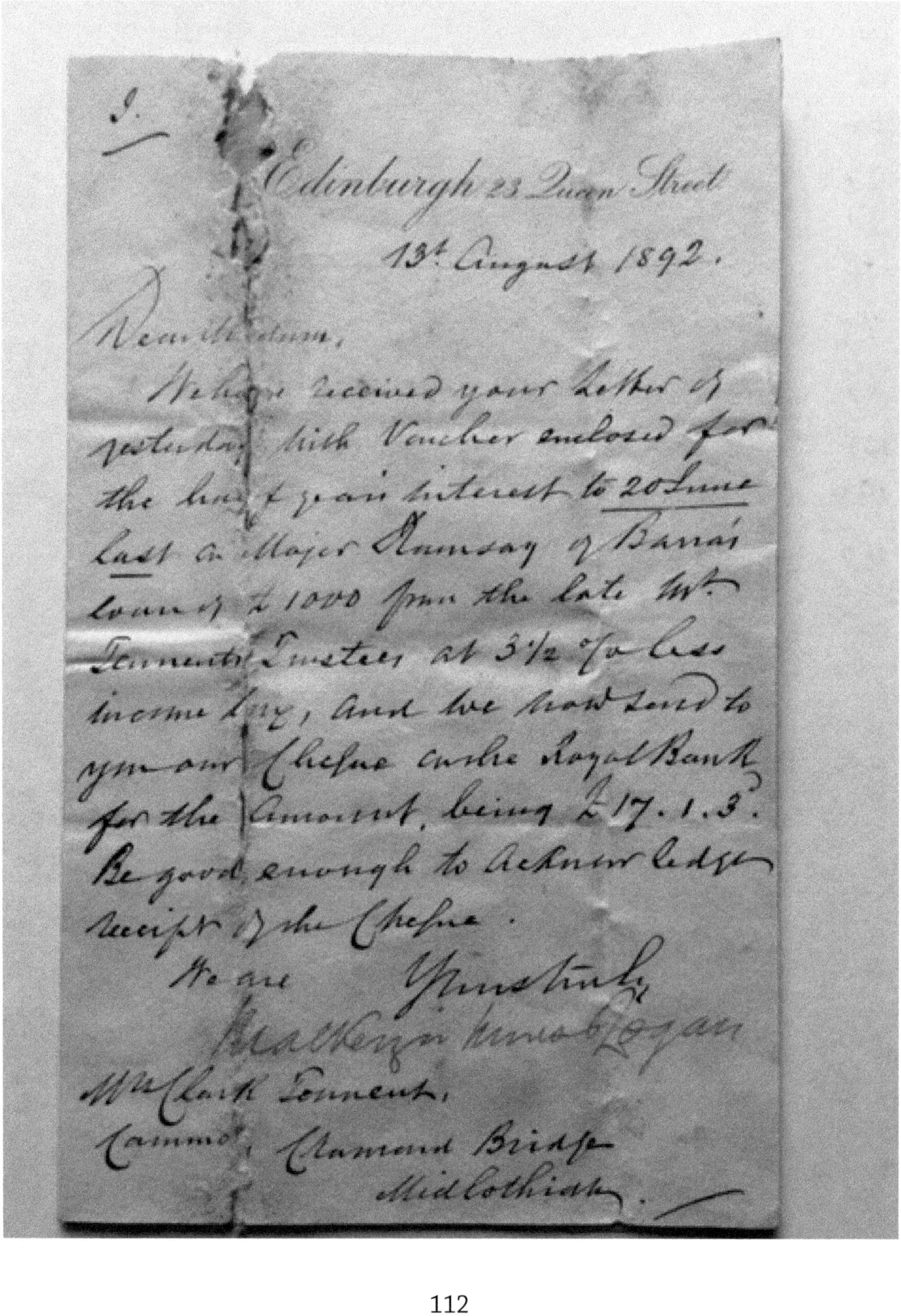

Edinburgh 23 Queen Street

13th August 1892.

Dear Madam,

We have received your letter of
yesterday with Voucher enclosed for
the half year's interest to 20 June
last on Major Ramsay of Barra's
loan of £1000 from the late Mr.
Tennent's Trustees at 3½ % less
income tax, And we now send to
you our Cheque on the Royal Bank
for the Amount, being £17.1.3.
Be good enough to acknowledge
receipt of the Cheque.

We are   Yours truly,

Walker, Kerr & Logan

Mrs Clark Tennent,
Cammo, Cramond Bridge
Mid Lothian.

THE LIVERPOOL & LONDON & GLOBE INSURANCE COMPANY,

1, DALE STREET,

LIVERPOOL, 16th _____ 1893

APPENDIX   PARTICULARS

OF THE

ESTATE OF CAMMO,

INCLUDING THE

FARM OF BRAEHEAD MAINS,

IN THE

COUNTY OF MIDLOTHIAN.

THE RESIDENTIAL ESTATE OF **CAMMO** and FARM OF **BRAE-HEAD MAINS** are situated five miles west of Edinburgh, on the banks of the River Almond, in one of the most picturesque

CAMMO HOUSE.

localities in Midlothian. It is reached by the Queensferry Road, one of the finest highways in the kingdom, Cammo House lying about half a mile off the main Road. There is also an Avenue over three quarters of a mile in length, leading to the Linlithgow Road, in addition to accesses to the cross Roads between the Queensferry and the Linlithgow Roads.

THE MANSION-HOUSE contains four Public Rooms, Smoking and Billiard Room, fourteen Bedrooms, Bathroom, &c., Laundry, Washhouse, and ample Servants' accommodation. Hot and Cold Water is laid on through the House.

The House, Stables, and Garden are supplied by Water from a Tower situated near the Stables, and a supply of Soft Water is laid on to the House and Stables from a Pond near the House. The Edinburgh Water has recently been introduced into Braehead Farm-House and Steading, and the Pipe could easily be extended to the Mansion-House.

The House, which is situated in finely laid-out Policy and Pleasure Grounds, commands beautiful views of the Pentland and Corstorphine Hills, and the Firth of Forth can be seen from the upper windows.

The Furniture, which is good, may be had at valuation.

VIEW OF THE HOUSE FROM THE POND.

THE PARK contains a variety of old and beautiful Trees, many of them nearly 200 years old, and the other growing Wood on the Estate is valuable. There are beautiful Walks along the banks of the River Almond, which bounds the Property, and is adorned by splendid Timber.

There is a **FLOWER GARDEN** and Lawn, with a Pond, well adapted for Curling, and enclosed Shrubbery of 8 Acres close to the House, and the **WALLED GARDEN** of 2½ Acres, containing Vineries, Peach-House, and Conservatory, is at a short distance.

There is a **ROOKERY** on the Property.

The **STABLES** contain ten Stalls and two Loose Boxes, and accommodation for six Carriages. The other Offices consist of Byre, Piggery, Fowl-House, Wright's Shop, Tool-House, and Fruit Store, with Lofts, Cart Shed, and Coalhouse.

There is a **Lodge** at the North Entrance, and a **Gardener's House, Coachman's House, Groom's Room,** and **Bothy** near the Stables.

The Mansion-House (furnished), with the Stables and Offices, Gardens and Pleasure-Grounds, with the Avenue Park, and two Paddocks south of the Garden, and Plantations along the River Almond and Bughtlin Burn, with the right of Shooting on the Lands of Cammo and

VIEW ON THE RIVER ALMOND.

Braehead Mains, are let to Mr. D. B. CLARK TENNENT, at the Rent of £220, the Tenant keeping up the House and Grounds.

The Linlithgow and Stirlingshire Hounds hunt the District, and the Kennels are within easy distance. The House was for several years occupied by the Master of the Hounds.

An excellent **Golf Course** has recently been opened on the Barnton Estate, about a mile distant from the House.

Cramond Brig Station is within a mile of the House, and the journey by rail to Edinburgh only occupies twenty minutes. The Estate therefore combines the rare advantages of a retired Country Residence with proximity to the Capital.

Cramond Bridge **Telegraph Office** is situated on the Property a little over half a mile from the Mansion-House, and close to Braehead Mains Farm-House.

The **POLICY GROUNDS and WOODS** extend to about **120** Acres in all, and consist of Pasture, Pleasure-Grounds, and Plantations. The Pasture within the Policy Grounds proper is let annually as Grass Parks.

VIEW OF THE HOUSE FROM THE VISTA PARK.

Mr. GRAY, the Tenant of Braehead Mains, has agreed to take a Lease of the **SHEEP PARK**, extending to **26·711** Acres Imperial, on a Lease for five years from Martinmas 1895, at the Rent of £85, under an obligation to lay down and leave the Park in Grass.

The remaining Cammo Parks outside the Policies, extending to **61·074** Acres, are let to Mr. GRAY, along with Braehead Mains, as after mentioned.

The **FARM OF BRAEHEAD MAINS,** along with certain of the Cammo Parks, is let on Lease to Mr. JAMES GRAY, one of the best known Farmers in the Lothians, on a Lease for nineteen years from Martinmas and separation of Crop 1895, with power to Proprietors or Tenant to terminate the Lease, either as regards the whole or any part of the subjects let, on giving notice in writing two years prior to any term of Martinmas during the Lease.

The Rent under the Lease is **£530.** The extent of Braehead Mains, according to the new Ordnance Survey Sheets, is **71·398** Imperial Acres, whereof **68·988** Acres are Arable, the remainder consisting of Steading, &c.; and the extent of the Cammo Parks, included in the Lease, is **61·074** Acres.

AVENUE FROM NORTH ENTRANCE.

The Land is of excellent quality and is in a high state of cultivation. It is conveniently served by Public Roads, which facilitates the disposal of Grass and Green Crops. The Farm and District have been long famed in connection with the production of early Potatoes.

There is an excellent **Farm-House,** forming a desirable Residence, and the Steading is commodious.

6   *Particulars of the Estate of Cammo.*

There are admirable **SITES FOR FEUS**, commanding Views of the Firth of Forth, the Pentland Hills, and surrounding Country, and sheltered from the east by Corstorphine Hill.

The Lands of Cammo (formerly called New Saughton) and Braehead Mains are situated in the Parish of Cramond; the Four-Mile Hill Park is in the Parish of Corstorphine. Cammo holds blench of the Crown for payment of a nominal Feu-Duty, if asked only. Braehead Mains holds of a subject-superior; Feu-Duty One Shilling Scots, at which sum the entry of heirs and singular successors is taxed. The Teinds of Braehead Mains are valued.

A **Rental of the Estate** is appended, with a note of the Burdens, and a Plan will be exhibited to intending Purchasers.

These Particulars, Rental, Extent, and Plan, though believed to be correct, are not guaranteed, and intending Purchasers must satisfy themselves before making Offers.

Further particulars can be obtained from Messrs. J., C., & A. STEUART, W.S., 17 India Street, Edinburgh, who have the Titles.

Cammo House Inventory 1897

1. North-west bedroom

Grate, wire fireguard, fender, fire-irons, papered coalbox, two canopies, candleflash, two blinds, carpet, three birch chairs, wardrobe, washstand, one basin, square washcloth, chest of drawers, toilet table, glass, iron bed, straw pillows, hair mattress, bolster, one pillow, two single blinds, white couch.

2. South-west bedroom

Grate, fireguard, fender, fire-irons, candlestick, two canopies, pole for window, damask curtains, two blinds, carpet, rug, birch armchair, basin and stand, two basins, bottle green couch, inkstand and bottle, pillow and cushion, toilet table, pin tray, chest of drawers, two chairs, small round folding table, wardrobe, iron bed, white couch, spring mattress, bolster and pillow, two blankets.

3. South-middle bedroom

Grate, blower, fender, fire-irons, chintz curtains, wardrobe, folding chair, square wardrobe, cushion, toilet table with drawers, glass, chair, towel stand, basin etc., bottle tumbler, painted stop pail and cover, iron bed, straw pillow, hair mattress, three simple cushions, blankets and blinds, white couch, bolster and pillows, carpet, rug, linen basket.

4. South-east bedroom

Grate, fireguard, fender, two sets pink tweed window curtains, two sets of lace curtains, carpet and rug, wardrobe, birch folding chair, pine table, chest of drawers, toilet table, potstand, iron folding chair, iron bed, three cushions and pillows, basinstand, two basins, bottle tumbler, square wardrobe, spring mattress, hair mattress, bolster, two pillows, two blinds, two chairs, towel rail.

5. West bedroom

Grate, fender, fire-irons, two firescreens, iron bed, curtains, one blind, carpet and rug, square wardrobe, skin mat, two chairs, toilet table, mirror, one washstand and basin, one bottle, chest of drawers, potstand, straw pillow, hair mattress, bolster and pillow, three single key blankets.

6. North bedroom

Grate, fender, fire-irons, carpet, rug, chest of drawers, one chair, can chair, basin and stand, iron bed, straw pillow, hair mattress, bolster and pillow, two single key blankets.

7. North-east bedroom

Grate, fireguard, fender, fire-irons, coalbox, two candlesticks, pole for window, chintz curtains, carpet, wardrobe, rug, basinstand, two basins, bottle tumbler, eye bath, folding chair, two chairs, toilet table, iron bed, straw pillow, hair mattress, bolster and pillow, three single key blankets, white couch.

8. Top landing

Mats, fire bucket, oil painting.

9. Bedroom (with roof light)

Grate, wire fireguard, fender, fire-irons, two heat screens, two candlesticks, bottle and stopper, engraving, damask curtains, lace curtains, carpet and rug, two chairs, couch, Sutherland table, old table cover, toilet table, wardrobe, linen basket, two potstands, double basin and stand, bottle tumbler, foot bath, easy chair, iron bed, spring mattress, hair mattress, bolster and pillows, three single key blankets.

10. Bedroom (with roof light)

Grate, fender, fire-irons, firescreen, carpet, rug, skin mat, square wardrobe, chest of drawers, bottle and glass tumbler, chair, night stove, bed, straw pillow, hair mattress, bolster, two pillows, four single key blankets.

11. Housemaid's closet

Three fire buckets, seven hot water cans, one painted fender, housemaids' broom, carpet switch, dustpan (no handle), one old candlestick.

12. Bathroom

Two keys for door, one chair, one chamber, sponge bucket, thermometer, soap dish, flesh brush, water mixer.

13. Spare bedroom (unused)

Grate, fireguard, fender, fire-irons, carpet, square wardrobe, two mahogany chairs, basin and stand, potstand, mahogany washstand, two basins, bottle tumbler, towel rail, bolster and bedstead, mahogany table.

14. Spare bedroom (unused)

Grate, fireguard, fender, fire-irons, carpet, square wardrobe, two mahogany chairs, basin and stand, potstand, mahogany washstand, two basins, bottle tumbler, towel rail, bolster and bedstead, mahogany table.

15. Small bedroom (no. 7)

Grate, fireguard, fire-irons and shovel, candlestick, engraving, square wardrobe, basin and stand, one basin, bottle and tumbler, birch toilet table, potstand, birch bed, straw pillow, bolster and pillow, three single key blankers, white couch.

16. Bedroom (above parlour)

Grate, wire fireguard, fire-irons, one candlestick, old black skin rug, iron basinstand, painted footbath, chamber, water bottle, chain seat for me, chest of drawers, iron bed, straw pillows, hair mattress, bolster and pillow, two single key blankets, white couch.

17. Landing and stair

Grate, carpet, wire fireguard, fire-irons, six oil paintings, two chairs.

18. North-east servant's bedroom

Grate, fender, fire-irons, iron bed, wardrobe, mirror, coloured bed linen, chest of drawers, washstand, basin, straw and feather pillows.

19. South-east servant's bedroom

Grate, fender, fire-irons, iron bed, wardrobe, mirror, coloured bed linen, chest of drawers, washstand, basin, straw and feather pillow.

20. Landing to drawing room

Three engravings, grate, fireguard, two metal urns, fire-irons.

21. Ante-drawing room

Grate, fire-irons, coalbox, two firescreens, taper holder, oil painting, two flip wall brackets, old china, two pairs tapestry curtains, lace curtains, carpet, ottoman, walnut cabinet, writing desk, two walnut chairs covered in mixed damask, flower stand, piano stool, writing table, table cloth, wicker chair, footstool, walnut easy chair, two damask chairs, walnut couch, feather pillow, metronome, mahogany table with drawers and folding leaf, mahogany book tray.

22. Drawing room

Grate, fire-irons, two china vases with raised flowers, pinch china basket, four photos in frames, five crystal brackets with drops, five pairs lace curtains, carpet tapestry rug and mats, two skin mats, coalbox, footstool, ebony table, bed table cover, walnut couch, cushioned bolster and pillow, two papier-mâché firescreens, pillow and bolster, sand glass stool, davenport, papier-mâché inkstand, mahogany what-not, lady's easy chair in red walnut, five chairs in red damask, walnut inlaid table on pillar and writing desk with reading lamp, round wicker table, walnut arm chair, pinewood card table, tapestry over dado, china vase, blue crystal vase, white china vase, walnut Sutherland table, walnut hall seat in red damask, ebony corner chair with willow seat, walnut cabinets, round walnut fly table, mahogany inlaid card table with folding leaf, three semicircular crystal majolica flower vases on feet, brown gilt davenport, two blue painted flower vases, walnut lady's chair, walnut and inlaid table on blocks, crystal flower case, fluted flower vase, round walnut fly table on pillar and block with cover, walnut lady's easy chair.

23. Library
Grate, fender, fire-irons, coalbox, two red stone bases, two black candlesticks, engraving, carpet, eight water-colours, 277 books, four oak chairs, walnut couch, pedestal mahogany table with drawers, large oak Sutherland table with green cloth cover, walnut easy chair, mahogany fly table, pillow and bolster.

24. Smoking room
Grate, ashpan, walnut fire fender, photo in oak frame, oak easy chair in red morocco leather, ashtray, folding birch table, mahogany inland table with drawers, mahogany bookcase, ash folding table and chair, carpet seat, pitch pine couch in morocco leather.

25. Dining room
Grate, fire-irons, coalbox, two candlesticks and match holders, oil lamp with opaque shade, 14 engravings, thermometer, two sets curtains, carpet, 14 oak chairs, table and sideboard, potstand, firescreen, mahogany table, tapestry, walnut stool in tapestry, oak sideboard, two wicker chairs, back screen round mahogany fly table on pillar and claws, mahogany sofa, bolster, basket chair, two cushions, Japanese fly screen.

26. Store cupboard
Set of steps etc.

27. Butler's pantry
Cloths etc. for silver, fire bucket.

28. Billiard room
Grate, fire-irons, fender, fireguard, pheasant, hawk, bronze, 21 oil paintings, four water-colours, deer horns, metal foot scraper, Indian mat, bush mat, carpet, six teacups, bracket and lamp, billiard ball washing bowl, metal umbrella stand, three chairs in red cloth, 21 antique chairs, two spittoons, cue stand, 15 cues, two long cues, two rests, one long rest, one small walnut ball bucket, mahogany straight edge, two beech folding chairs, wicker chair, two tapestry chairs, rosewood inlaid table, 27 ivory balls, one Japanese papier-mâché firescreen, mahogany side-table with white marble top, cue tip cleaner, oak ball bucket, bronze.

29. Parlour
Grate, fender, fire-irons, fireguard, stool, two majolica vases, two sets of curtains, four engravings, carpet, bookcase, walnut armchair in damask, lady's chair, elmwood tea caddy on pedestal, six walnut chairs, spittoon, oak cabinet, walnut sofa, feather pillow, round mahogany loo table, tapestry chair, blotting pad, 481 books.

30. Cloakroom
Grate, wire fireguard, carpet, two chairs, bottle tumbler, coat stand.

31. Wash house
Wash basins, washing machine, two loosecloth tubs, coal shovel, steps, soap pan, foot board, line and pegs.

32. Laundry
Ironing tables, one clothes horse, tub.

33. Servants' hall
Grate, iron fender, two bookshelves, tables with drawers (white), two wicker chairs, one hardwood chair.

34. Kitchen

Range, smoke board, fender, kettle and cover, toasting bracket, hot plate, coal shovel, coal scuttle, 25 serving dishes, four shelves, three brass jelly pans, round tin pan and cover, tin steamer, colander, six jelly shapes, ice mould, seven dish covers, tin cheese grater, tin measure, tin sugar dredge, weighing machine and six weights (brass), two dozen tea trays, mortar and pestle, 12 skewers, two meat hooks, desser, five wooden spoons, four hangers and hooks, sardine pan, potato beater, mincing knife, meat baster, urn heater, two cook's knives, iron ladle, tin fish slice, ice spade, egg switch, pewter tankard, oak table, two lemon squeezers, 12 white-handled fish knives, 12 white-handled meat knives, salt spoon, six oil lamps, water tower key, brass melon jelly shape, six round cake pans, four spice jars, tin coffee pot, plate warmer, game table with two drawers, vegetable cutter, 12 tin cake moulds, ten tin pastry pans, ten fluted pastry pans, ten pastry cutters, six small tin pastry pans, two flower vases, two chairs, housemaid's broom, two rusted ladles, tin roasting tray, tin fish pan, wine decanter, lemon juicer, baking board, ten Bristol cans, five covers, eight big tablespoons, ten big dessert spoons, six teaspoons, one saltspoon, four bone china egg cups, tablecloth, two wooden egg cups.

35. Scullery

Seven crystal goblets, mincing board, two dozen saucepans, three frying pans, one fluted pudding dish, old basin.

36. Larder

Bread can, pair of steps.

37. Low passage and cellars

Key for back door, two archery targets, oil lamp, sow's head brush, two old door mats, one old stool, 12 garden urns and clay pots.

The facade of the stables, 2017. SJB

Eastern side of the stables, 2017. SJB

Original cobble setts in situ at the stables, 2017. SJB

The water tower with the man-made knowle in the background, 2017. SJB

The walled garden gate piers, 2017. SJB

Evidence of the enormous glasshouse against the 18th century garden wall, 2017. SJB

The devastating demolition, 1978. DM

*The sundial adjacent to Mrs Maitland-Tennent's
grave, February 1976. DM*

HES historic environment Scotland

NTS national trust for Scotland

SJB Simon John Baillie

DM Douglas Mickel

EAFS Edinburgh archaeology field society

JP Johnston press

CPSIA information can be obtained
at www.ICGtesting.com
Printed in the USA
BVHW022016010119
536770BV00016B/311/P

9 781912 850273